THE DEAF MUTE
HOWLS

GALLAUDET CLASSICS IN DEAF STUDIES

A SERIES EDITED BY
John Vickrey Van Cleve

THE DEAF MUTE
HOWLS

Albert Ballin

INTRODUCTION BY

Douglas C. Baynton

Gallaudet University Press

WASHINGTON, D.C.

GALLAUDET CLASSICS IN DEAF STUDIES

A SERIES EDITED BY
John Vickrey Van Cleve

The photographs used in this edition are reproduced from the original
edition courtesy of the Gallaudet University Archives. Additional
photographs used courtesy of the Gallaudet University Archives.

Gallaudet University Press
Washington, D.C. 20002

10 09 08 07 06 05 04   5 4 3 2

Library of Congress Cataloging-in-Publication Data

Ballin, Albert, 1861–
    The deaf mute howls / Albert Ballin : introduction by Douglas C.
Baynton.
        p.   cm.—(Gallaudet classics in deaf studies)
    Originally published: Los Angeles, Calif. : Grafton Pub. Co.,
c 1930.
    Includes bibliographical references.
    ISBN 1-56368-073-4 (alk.paper)
        1. Ballin, Albert, 1861– . 2. Deaf men—United States—
Biography.   3. Deaf—Means of communication—United States.
4. Sign Language—United States. I. Title. II. Series.
HV1624.B354A3   1998
342.4'2'092—dc21
    [B]   98-38153
                                                     CIP

♾ The paper used in this publication meets the minimum
requirements of American National Standard for Information
Sciences—Permanence of Paper for Printed Library
Materials, ANSI Z39.48-1984.

DEDICATION

To that "humanity of man" that loves
best and serves most, and should know
the Deaf-Mute's problems and what
his knowledge can impart to world
progress that we may all together lift
humanity to a higher standard

CONTENTS

CONTENTS

ILLUSTRATIONS

EDITOR'S PREFACE

WITH THE PUBLICATION of Albert Ballin's *The Deaf Mute Howls*, Gallaudet University Press inaugurates a new series, Gallaudet Classics in Deaf Studies. The series will make available modern editions of historically significant works that inform a social understanding of the culture and experiences of deaf people. Each author's style and meaning will be preserved as the texts are made accessible to today's readers. New introductions, written for the Gallaudet Classics edition of each book, will place these works in their historical and intellectual context, such as the turbulent period through which Albert Ballin, a deaf artist and actor and the son of a deaf engraver, lived.

Ballin's book is angry, yet humorous and optimistic. Ballin hoped that *The Deaf Mute Howls* would allow the hearing world to see inside deaf culture and to understand deaf people's need for unfettered visual communication. He believed that hearing people would appreciate his insights as he described the experiences deaf people confront in education and in daily life. And he thought that hearing readers would welcome his suggestions for learning sign language.

Ballin was disappointed, though, as historian Douglas C. Baynton writes in his introduction. Ballin's book, originally published in 1931, sold few copies, and hearing people in his day neither learned to sign nor were willing to listen to deaf persons. American society has changed since the original publication of *The Deaf Mute Howls*. It may now be ready to hear Ballin's message.

JOHN VICKREY VAN CLEVE
Director, Gallaudet University Press
Professor of History, Gallaudet University

INTRODUCTION

Douglas C. Baynton

ALBERT BALLIN, a deaf artist and writer, lived a life of many ambitions. His greatest ambition was that the publication of his book, *The Deaf Mute Howls*, would transform not only education for deaf children but also the relationship between deaf and hearing people everywhere. Ballin believed the book offered an answer—a sovereign "Remedy" as he called it—for the ills that afflicted deaf people living in a mostly hearing world. While his primary concern was to improve the lot of the typical deaf person, "shunned and isolated as a useless member of society," he was convinced that his Remedy would enrich the lives of hearing people as well, perhaps even helping to bring about international understanding and world peace. His Remedy was this: to instruct all people, hearing and deaf, in sign language.

Our knowledge of Ballin's life is sketchy. Though he writes in the first person in *The Deaf Mute Howls*, he tells us at the beginning that when he recounts his school years he is writing in the persona of a composite, or "typical" deaf person. Some of what he says applies to him, but some does not, and it is difficult to tell where Ballin ends and the composite begins.

Born in 1861, Ballin became deaf at the age of three, but presum-

Douglas C. Baynton, author of *Forbidden Signs: American Culture and the Campaign against Sign Language* (University of Chicago Press, 1996), is an assistant professor of history and American Sign Language at the University of Iowa.

ably not from scarlet fever (as he states in *The Deaf Mute Howls*) since his father, David Ballin, had also become deaf at an early age. A skilled lithographer, the elder Ballin had emigrated from Germany to the United States at the age of twenty-two and established a successful engraving business in New York, which he held in partnership with his sons until his death. When Ballin writes that his parents "had never heard of the existence of deaf people before" and had never learned sign language, he is clearly not speaking of himself but rather of the typical parent of a deaf child. We also know that his lament that the "nerve centers that would make me capable of understanding a spoken or written language . . . deteriorated and became atrophied from disuse" was not true of him. Indeed, Ballin not only wrote for the deaf press and other magazines and newspapers, but his obituary notes "his life-long habit in mastering one foreign language after another" as well as his enjoyment of books written in French, Italian, and Spanish.[1] He apparently spoke and lip-read relatively well.[2] He was also known for a creative eloquence in ASL and a mastery of pantomime. He attended the New York School for the Deaf, studied painting in New York with H. Humphrey Moore, a well-known deaf painter of the time, and spent three years in Rome studying with the Spanish painter Jose Villegas. Ballin had some early success, winning a silver medal for one of his paintings in 1882 in Rome and an honorable mention the following year in Munich.[3] Unable, however, to make a living at painting, he entered his father's lithography business while in his twenties.[4] He also taught sign language, was active for a time in Democratic Party politics, and earned extra income lecturing to deaf audiences.[5] Later in life he tried to make a living as an actor in Hollywood.

Why does he adopt the "composite" persona rather than write as himself? Ballin's purpose is to depict what becomes of the average deaf student in America. He knew that he was an unusually successful student, especially in English and oral communication, the two most emphasized and problematic areas of study for deaf

Albert Victor Ballin

students. He was relatively privileged. Of his mother I could find no record, but his father was not only a skilled craftsman with his own business, he was also deaf. Deaf children with at least one deaf parent tend to have better communication skills both in sign language and English and are generally more socially adept and confident than those raised by hearing parents. Because they associate with other deaf people from an early age, they begin acquiring language, social skills, and general knowledge earlier; they learn strategies for communicating with hearing people; and, in short, they learn how to be deaf in a mostly hearing world from those with experience at it. Since 90 percent of deaf children have hearing parents, Ballin's own experiences in school do not suit his purpose in *The Deaf Mute Howls,* which is to illustrate the effects of the current educational system on the majority of deaf children.

Ballin has two chief targets in his criticism of deaf education: the philosophy of "pure oralism" (the sole use of oral communication without sign language or fingerspelling) that was then dominant in the schools for deaf children and the practice of educating deaf students apart from hearing students. While Ballin's dislike for residential schools sets him apart from most deaf commentators, his condemnation of oralism places him well in the mainstream. Indeed, though he remarks that some people had criticized the harshness of his rhetoric, he was in fact one of a long line of deaf people to denounce oralism in similar terms. Joseph Schuyler Long, for example, in 1890 charged that "Chinese women bind their babies' feet to make them small; the Flathead Indians bind their babies' heads to make them flat. And the people who prevent the sign language being used in the education of the deaf . . . are in the same class of criminals."[6] The first president of the National Association of the Deaf, Robert McGregor, asked rhetorically, in 1896, "By whom then are signs proscribed?" He answered, "By a few educators of the deaf whose boast is that they do not understand signs and do not want to; by a few philanthropists who are otherwise ignorant of the language; by parents who do not understand the requisites to the happiness of their deaf children and are inspired with false fears by the educators and philanthropists."[7] Such condemnations continued throughout the twentieth century. In 1974, when the tide had begun to turn against the dominance of oralism, deaf writers such as Leo Jacobs were still condemning the "reprehensible" and "repressive" teaching methods that left deaf children "deprived of meaningful communication" (the title of his 1974 book, *A Deaf Adult Speaks Out*, seems to be a more temperate echo of Ballin's title). Ballin was but one of a long line of deaf community leaders to denounce oralism during the long years of its ascendance.

The Suppression of Sign Language

While the story of the campaign against sign language is familiar to most deaf people, few hearing people are aware of it. Insofar as the goal was to eliminate the use of sign language among deaf people, it was largely a failure. Sign language continued to be passed down from generation to generation and to be the primary language of the great majority of deaf people. However, the campaign did succeed in banishing sign language from most classrooms in schools for deaf students for the better part of a century, a success that would have a profound effect on the education of generations of deaf children.

The campaign was also successful in bringing to an end the scholarly study of American Sign Language (ASL) that had begun in the nineteenth century. As a consequence, there are many popular misconceptions about ASL, despite the resurgence of interest in the language in recent decades. For example, the common assumption that there is one universal sign language often coexists with the contradictory and equally erroneous belief that ASL is a manual code for English invented for educating deaf children. Still today, few are aware that it is a natural language that has evolved, just as spoken languages do, within a linguistic community, or that like other languages it is governed by grammatical rules unique to itself. ASL is often confused with the more limited and cumbersome manually coded English systems invented for the purpose of teaching English to deaf children. These are artificial codes, not true languages.[8]

It was not understood until recently that the sign languages of the world constitute distinct languages. Due to a happenstance of history, ASL is closely related to French Sign Language (FSL), and while ASL and FSL have diverged considerably over the years, they remain mutually intelligible to some extent.[9] British Sign Language and ASL, on the other hand, are quite distinct (as Ballin makes clear, however, it is far easier to bridge the gap between different sign languages than it is between spoken languages—largely because of the proficiency with gesture and pantomime that most signers develop).

The close relation of FSL and ASL came about in 1817, when the Reverend Thomas H. Gallaudet established the first school for deaf people in the United States, the American Asylum for the Deaf and Dumb, in Hartford, Connecticut.[10] The school's head teacher, Laurent Clerc, was a deaf man who had been a student and subsequently a teacher at the Royal Institute for the Deaf and Dumb in Paris. Clerc brought to Hartford the sign language of Paris, a city with a large deaf community and a sophisticated sign language, both of which had been in existence since at least the late eighteenth century.[11] Clerc taught this sign language to Gallaudet and his fellow teachers, and it became the official language of the school.

The United States was a rural country with no great cities like Paris, but it nevertheless had at least one well-developed sign language at the start of the nineteenth century. On Martha's Vineyard, from the seventeenth to the nineteenth century, an unusually high rate of inherited deafness resulted in a community in which both hearing and deaf islanders knew and used a signed language. Though most of the deaf students at Hartford came from rural areas and learned at school how to communicate via language rather than pantomime and gesture, some came from Martha's

Vineyard and brought with them the sign language of the island. Modern ASL was formed from the encounter of this and possibly other indigenous sign languages with FSL.[12]

The American Asylum was the first of many residential schools established around the country—within forty years of its establishment in 1817 there were twenty and by the turn of the century, more than fifty schools for deaf people. Thousands of young deaf people spent years living and studying together, the outcome of which was not just a new sign language but a new culture as well. Deaf people began to create cultural traditions and folklore that they handed down from generation to generation—stories, poetry, games, and jokes in ASL, as well as distinct naming practices, mores, and rules of etiquette. Most socialized and married within the deaf community. A deaf periodical press came into existence in the latter half of the nineteenth century, with dozens of newspapers such as *The Deaf-Mutes' Journal, The Jewish Deaf,* and *Silent Worker.* Deaf people established local clubs, state organizations, and, in 1880, the National Association of the Deaf. They attended churches where sign language was the medium of both sermon and song.[13]

In the years following the Civil War, many hearing people became increasingly uneasy about this developing culture and language. Prominent Americans such as Alexander Graham Bell, together with hearing educators and parents unhappy with their children's education, began to advocate the suppression of ASL in the schools in favor of the exclusive use of lipreading and speech. The debate was not merely over the provision of oral training. While all schools began adding training in speech and lipreading to their curricula and increasingly emphasized fingerspelling rather than sign language in the classroom, oralists opposed the use of manual communication in any form. You will notice that Ballin on occasion refers to these reformers as "pure oralists." Like most deaf people of the time, Ballin advocated what was termed the "combined system"—oral training proportionate to a child's ability to benefit from it, along with the use of fingerspelling and sign language. Although the great majority of deaf people fought against the oralist movement, deaf people did not control the schools. By 1920 nearly 80 percent of American deaf students were taught entirely without the use of sign language; deaf teachers, who had numbered nearly half of all teachers of deaf children in the 1860s, were almost entirely purged from the profession.[14]

Oralism

Like many others who have criticized or tried to explain oralism, Ballin cannot avoid contradictions. On the one hand he refers to oralists as "parasites who prey on the misfortunes of the deaf," charlatans who make "ridiculous" and "extravagant claims" and engage in "humbuggery" in order to "deceive and delude the indiscriminate and gullible public." On the other hand, he concedes "a high motive and perfect honesty of purpose to some of the oralists." (Of course, immediately following this he further concedes that the same might be said of inquisitors, witch hunters, and heretic burners.) Of Alexander Graham Bell—whom Ballin considered a good friend despite their opposing views—he writes: "he was a prince of good fellows, and intended to be a friend of the deaf." Oralism is a great evil, but not oralists, and he is unable to reconcile the obvious sincerity and honest intentions of the advocates of oralism (many of whom, after all, were parents of deaf children) with the great harm he believed they were doing to deaf people or their blithe unwillingness to heed the opinions of deaf adults.

With a Manichaean desire for moral clarity, most of us prefer tales of heroes and villains. As Ballin knew, the oralists were neither. He does, however, depict oralists as a small minority who were prejudiced against sign language, and he addresses his plea for help to "you," the general reader, one of the good-hearted and unprejudiced (though perhaps uninformed) majority. This conveys a mistaken impression. Who were the oralists, and how were they different from the "you" Ballin wants to address? By all indications they were quite typical hearing people—not fanatics, not narrow-minded chauvinists bent on the oppression of deaf people, but ordinary reformers representative of the ordinary majority. Oralism was not a narrow phenomenon at all, but rather an expression of broad developments in American and Western culture.

In a humorous scene that Ballin invents, an oralist teacher upbraids a police officer for using gestures to direct traffic. The teacher uses the kind of convoluted, academic language Ballin associates with those more concerned with theories than with the real world. The teacher represents abstract, ivory-tower academic theory while the Irish officer is the soul of practicality—he had to stop a car and gestures suited the purpose. Among the teacher's long-winded remarks is this description of sign language: "those inconvertible, brain-corroding gesticulations of our pre-historical anthropophagic antecedents from whom we are supposed to have descended." In this parody of oralist rhetoric, Ballin hits upon a powerful reason for the widespread and implacable opposition to sign language at the time of oralism's ascendance.

The central cultural divide that separated the generations of teachers who used sign language from later teachers who opposed it was the rise of evolutionary theory. Most manualist teachers were of the generation that came of age before the publication of Charles Darwin's 1859 *Origin of Species*. The manualists' worldview was constructed on the theory of immediate creation, while the oralists' was built on an evolutionary understanding of the world. By the 1870s evolutionary analogies, explanations, and ways of thinking were ubiquitous, one result of which was a radical change in attitudes toward language—specifically toward the relative status of spoken and gesture languages.[15]

The origin of language was an important topic of philosophical discussion in both Europe and America throughout the eighteenth and nineteenth centuries, with many speculating that humans had used gestural language prior to spoken language.[16] As experts in sign language, the early American teachers of the deaf were naturally interested in this idea. Most were evangelical Protestants, many of them ministers, and they interpreted this theory in light of biblical history, in which humanity was created in its present form. Rather than the modern notion of an ever-evolving humanity, the creationist imagination was dominated by the story of the Fall from Grace. The theory that sign language preceded speech did not therefore imply inferiority. Instead, the antiquity of sign language suggested its superiority over modern, degenerate languages. It meant that sign language was "in the designs of Providence, the necessary forerunner of speech"—which for these teachers was a mark of honor.[17]

Later in the century, however, oralists interpreted the theory quite differently. If to the earlier generation "original language" meant "closer to the Creation," to post-Darwin oralists it meant "closer to the apes." In this evolutionary worldview, humanity had *risen* rather than fallen, and was the end product of history rather than its beginning. Antiquity was no mark of honor, but rather one of inferiority. Sign language was transformed into a language low on the evolutionary scale, antedating even the most "savage" spoken language.

Language scholars argued that inferior languages were continually being eliminated and replaced by superior ones in the "struggle for existence," formulating what was called "linguistic Darwinism." Sign language had suffered an early defeat in the struggle, it was said, and was now increasingly identified as a "savage" form of communication. Educators echoed the notion that sign language was "characteristic of tribes low in the scale of development," and that the sign language of deaf people "resembles the languages of the North American Indian and the Hottentot of South Africa." They believed that "as man emerged from savagery he discarded gestures for the expression of his ideas," and that therefore it was time that deaf people discarded them as well. They declared that spoken language was the "crown of history" and that to permit deaf children the use of sign language was to "push them back in the world's history to the infancy of our race."[18]

Sign language came to signify not only the supposedly inferior human but also the nonhuman. Speech was uniquely human, while "in the apes the gesture-language alone was developed."[19] Deaf people found themselves defending sign language against charges that it was nothing more than "a set of monkey-like grimaces and antics." They frequently encountered the insult, "You look like monkeys when you make signs," and complained of attempts to "impress [deaf people] with the thought that it is apish to talk on the fingers." Oralists scoffed that "these signs can no more be called a language than the different movements of a dog's tail and ears which indicate his feelings."[20]

Furthermore, hearing Americans were especially prone to distrust and oppose the use of languages other than English at this time. Earlier in the century, educators had been chiefly concerned with the spiritual life of deaf people. As evangelical Protestants, they saw themselves as missionaries to deaf people cut off from the Christian gospel. They learned the sign language of deaf people, just as other missionaries learned the languages of American Indians, Africans, and the Chinese and went to preach among the heathen. Those of the oralist generation, however, were more concerned with national unity than with salvation. During the ardent nationalism that followed the Civil War, fueled in part by the fear that divisions within the nation were dangerous, educators and others began to express concern about the "clannishness" of deaf people. By the 1890s, with record levels of immigration and cities becoming patchworks of ethnic enclaves, the charge of clannishness gave way to the more ominous charge of "foreignness." Foreignness was a powerful metaphor for late nineteenth-century Americans. A rekindled nativism resounded with calls for immigration restriction and the proscription of languages other than English in the schools. The suggestion that sign language turned deaf people into foreigners was a compelling argument against it.

Education journal articles about deaf people began warning that they "must be made people of our language," attacking "the foreign language of signs" and insisting that "the English language must be made the vernacular of the deaf if they are not to become a class unto themselves—foreigners among their own countrymen." Indeed, oralists charged, "no gesturer can become an American" because their primary and native language would never be English; "the gesturer is, and always will remain, a foreigner."[21] Alexander Graham Bell described sign language as "essentially a foreign language" and maintained that "in an English speaking country like the United States, the English language, *and the English language alone,* should be used as the means of communication and instruction—at least in schools supported at public expense." In a letter drafted to send to a journal of deaf education, Bell objected that the use of sign language "in our public schools is contrary to the spirit and practice of American Institutions (as foreign immigrants have found out)." He added it was "un-American," but apparently thought better of it and crossed the word out.[22]

Bell was especially disturbed that, according to his research, the rate of intermarriage among deaf people was over 80 percent. This issue brought together for Bell the three great interests of his life: elocution, eugenics, and deaf education. He and his father before him had spent their lives studying the physiology of speech. He thought it possible to teach all deaf children to communicate orally and asserted this claim in a steady stream of letters and articles. He also worried that deafness was increasing. In an 1884 paper published by the National Academy of Sciences, Bell warned that intermarriage among deaf people was producing a "great calamity," the "formation of a deaf variety of the human race." The chief cause of this intermarriage was, he argued, "segregation for the purposes of education, and the use, as a means of communication, of a language which is different from that of the people." Bell's fear of a proliferating deafness was based upon a faulty understanding of the genetics of deafness. Marriages between deaf people on average do not produce greater numbers of deaf offspring than mixed hearing/deaf marriages. However, the image of a foreign, inbred, and expanding deaf community was a powerful factor in turning public and professional opinion against sign language.[23]

Raze the Schools

Ballin's opposition to oralism was just one aspect of his dissatisfaction with deaf education, however. The other and equally important part of Ballin's plan to transform deaf education—the elimination of separate schools for deaf students—was an opinion far less typical in the deaf community. Here he was in agreement with many oralists—indeed, he says the idea was first suggested to him by Alexander Graham Bell—and out of step with nearly all advocates of sign language. Ballin describes the drawbacks to institutional life, beginning with the anguish of parents leaving their child at a boarding school miles from home. He recounts the difficulties children often have adjusting to their new life among hundreds of other children of all ages. While some remember their first days at school as a time of liberation, when they first discovered sign language and other deaf people like themselves, Ballin remembers (or has his composite self remember) "the nauseating homesickness I went through! It made me so ill that I had to be taken to the hospital ward for two days." The inflexible rules entailed by institutional life were, as he says, "unavoidable, perhaps, because of the difficulties of preserving order," yet no doubt especially hard on someone of Ballin's independent and adventurous temperament.[24]

Ballin's most serious criticism, however, is that the segregation of deaf children—"one of the greatest wrongs inflicted on deaf children"—leads them to develop peculiarities, to be different from "normal" people. He tells us that his father removed him from the school for deaf students early to study art, which saved him from becoming a "confirmed dummy"—not a "dummy" in the sense of not speaking but in the sense of being noticeably unlike hearing people: "I began to perceive that I was different from them in endless ways. . . . I was a thorough-going dummy in my habits, behavior, ideas, language, character, outlook on life—all of which made me repulsive to my new acquaintances." Ballin acknowledges that his dislike of residential schools is unusual, and that deaf adults generally have fond memories of their alma mater, but rather than exploring these complications to his picture of the residential school, he resorts to a glib analogy to dismiss them: "If you keep anyone enslaved long enough he will eventually acquire an affection for his chains."

This unusual aspect of Ballin's thinking may well be related to the strength of both his ambitions and his disappointments. We hear in *The Deaf Mute Howls* and his other writings a persistent undertone of frustration, a desire to have accomplished more, to have done more, to have *been* more. While he won praise and at least one award for his painting while a young man, his art career apparently faded quickly.[25] His former teacher at the New York Institution, Weston Jenkins, wrote in 1904 that Ballin had "produced some interesting pieces—landscapes and genre pictures, but, for whatever reason, his work did not secure the success which his high achievement as a student seemed to warrant."[26] His life in middle age is obscure, but he seems to have busied himself with a combination of working in his father's lithography business, selling a few paintings, teaching sign language, writing occasionally, and lecturing to deaf audiences.

Later in life he tried his hand at acting. After living in Hollywood for a year, he wrote in the *Silent Worker* that "Hollywood, with its inexpressibly intriguing charms, has completely captured my soul and, without struggle, I yield to the alluring prospect of remaining here, her willing slave, to the end of my days." His time there was filled "with marvelous adventures and experiences, to review which puts my head in a whirl."[27] However, while he landed occasional work as an extra in films, he was unable to make a living from it. In 1928 he wrote that as an extra, "I never get enough to keep the wolf off my door," but that he "was still hopeful of something really good and prominent" coming along. (Even that possibility was soon snatched from him with the advent of sound motion

pictures or "talkies"—like the telephone, an instance of technologi-
cal progress that was precisely the opposite as far as deaf people
were concerned.) "Fortunately," he continued, "I can paint portraits
and I do get orders at odd intervals. I hope to do this business exclusively in the dim future when my ability in this direction should be
better known." Thus wrote the once-promising young artist, at the
age of 67, of his tenacious hopes for the future.[28]

A persistent theme in *The Deaf Mute Howls* and other writings
by Ballin is that he would have accomplished much more were it
not for the difficulty of communication with hearing people. Ballin
craved success, sought adventure, reveled in hobnobbing with celebrities. While his life was by most standards varied and adventurous, he was disappointed by it. He saw his opportunities narrowed,
the possibilities for a satisfying life constricted, by his deafness.
While active in the deaf community—he wrote for several deaf periodicals, belonged to deaf clubs, lectured to deaf audiences, visited
schools for deaf people to tell of his adventures, was a delegate to
the World's Congress of the Deaf in 1889 in Paris[29]—he wanted a
wider compass. When a friend went to Cuba to film the raising of
the USS *Maine,* Ballin "could do nothing but look on helplessly, and
feel depressed because of the handicap that prevented my participating." Once he was about to be hired as an actor, but was rejected
because he "could not hear the director's instructions. Thus, once
more, the poor dummy missed another opportunity." Ballin, who
wanted to become a successful artist, act in movies, write about
Hollywood celebrities, participate in political campaigns, and travel
the world, saw being deaf, in the time he was living, as a frustrat-
ing limitation.

The Dilemma and the Remedy

This, then, was the central dilemma of Ballin's life, and it is what
drives his reasoning in *The Deaf Mute Howls.* Difficulties of communication "stand as an unsurmountable barrier against free and equal
companionship" between deaf and hearing people. Since oral com-

munication is simply not practical for most deaf people, a decent education and a satisfying social life are made possible for them only through sign language. On the other hand, while sign language enables communication, it limits communication to those few who know it and tends to segregate deaf people from hearing people. It makes separate schools necessary, which causes deaf people to behave in "peculiar" ways—differently from hearing people—which further reinforces their isolation from the hearing world and limits the opportunities available to them.

The dilemma seems intractable. It has powered the heated debates over sign language among educators since the beginning of deaf education. Oralism was the remedy offered by hearing people. Let all deaf people learn to speak and lip-read and the gulf between deaf and hearing people will be bridged. This of course is what hearing people tend always to ask from deaf people, what nondisabled people have always wanted from disabled people, and indeed what majorities have always wanted from minorities—that they adjust, change, make the effort, surmount the barriers. If deaf people would just learn to converse with hearing people in the manner to which hearing people are accustomed, then the deaf community would be "restored to society."

Ballin describes an encounter he had with a hearing man with whom communication was awkward, and asks, "Whose fault is it—his or mine? It may now look like fifty-fifty to you." Doubtless he is too charitable toward his hearing readers. Oralism by definition claims it is not fifty-fifty, but instead assigns almost the entire responsibility to the deaf person to learn to communicate with the hearing—and most hearing people would probably agree. Ballin, however, will have none of that. To him, it is the hearing person's fault. He argues that deaf people can sacrifice years upon years in the quest for speech and lipreading, and still most will fall short. Any hearing person, especially if taught as a child, can learn to sign. Thus Ballin's "Remedy": let everyone learn sign language.

Ballin presents the only argument he can make given his premises. All other answers are partial and in some way work against the interests of deaf people. Oralism is a hearing society's fantasy, while segregated education with sign language creates limits that, to him, are intolerable. Everyone learning sign language is the only total solution.

Ballin claims a number of immediate benefits for deaf people if everyone knew sign language: (1) deaf children could attend public schools with hearing children; (2) by associating with hearing people, deaf people would better learn English and not develop "peculiar" ways; (3) hearing parents could teach their deaf children as they do their hearing children; and (4) deaf people could mingle with hearing people as equals and their "impediment would seldom be noticed." All careers, opportunities, and the world at large would at last be open to them.

Ballin and Bell

When Ballin told others of his idea, some dismissed it as "too Utopian," and indeed Ballin is best understood as a utopian thinker. His utopianism can perhaps account for his friendship with and obvious affection for Alexander Graham Bell, an altogether unlikely attraction between a champion of sign language and its leading opponent. Both were utopian thinkers who found appealing the idea of a clean slate and a new beginning, of one right answer and a single sovereign remedy. Bell exclaims: "[A]ll the schools for the deaf, both the combined and the pure oral, should be razed to the ground!" and Ballin responds, "Three Cheers for the Razing!" Despite their profoundly different positions on sign language, Ballin and Bell are similar types. Both are revolutionaries, ready to raze existing structures to make way for a better world.

If education via sign language at the residential schools was only a partial and imperfect answer, if it failed to provide a total solution to the difficulties of being deaf in a mostly hearing world, then for Ballin and Bell it was unsatisfactory and had to be overthrown. The one best system had to be found. For Bell it was oralism, for Ballin, universal knowledge of sign language. Bell and Ballin were in remarkable ways mirror images of one another. Bell wished to bridge the divide that separated the deaf from the hearing by bringing deaf people into his world. Ballin wanted to do the same thing by bringing hearing people into his. Ballin's hearing wife (who had grown up with deaf siblings) was fluent in sign language and was thus the embodiment of his ideal. Bell's deaf wife had been raised and lived her life entirely without sign language, and was thus the embodiment of *his* ideal.[30] Ballin sees the possibility of hearing people learning sign language in the example of his wife, and Bell sees the possibility of deaf people learning oral communication in the example of his wife. Utopian thinkers both, Ballin and Bell generalized from one example to the world at large.

Ballin's claim was not merely that a universal knowledge of sign language would benefit deaf people. It was far more sweeping than that. He begins by mentioning several trivial advantages—people could chat at the theater without bothering others; waiters could communicate without disturbing patrons; construction workers, firefighters, movie directors, and others who need to communicate in noisy places or at a distance would find it useful—but he presents a grander vision of how "the whole world would benefit." Reflecting the common belief at the time that sign language was essentially the same throughout the world, he argues that sign language could become an international language of commerce and diplomacy, a *lingua franca* as it once was for the American Plains Indians. With a universally understood sign language would come a "new understanding among all races and nations. . . . It will help to bring peace on the earth, and good will to man."

Ballin's attraction to utopian solutions is evident in ways large and small. He saw in the movies potential for "bringing about a universal brotherhood of man," and lamented that the invention of talkies would undermine that promise. In the 1890s he lectured to deaf audiences on the idea of the "single tax" (a tax on unearned income from land ownership advocated by utopian reformer Henry

George as a panacea for economic inequality). Even Ballin's invention of a "perpetual calendar" suggests the temperament of a man prone to seek ultimate answers—a universal calendar, a universal tax, a universal language. He sells his sign language idea with words reminiscent of the patent medicine advertisements of his day: "You may find comfort in the assurance that now there exists a REMEDY . . . a reliable cure for not only the troubles of the deaf but for others, of the afflicted of mankind."

Like his other ambitions, Ballin's dream of liberating humanity from the curse of Babel ended in disappointment. His book sold poorly and hardly at all outside of a small circle of deaf people. It sparked no movement to dismantle the residential schools for the deaf, to abandon oralism, or to teach sign language in the public schools. Two years after its publication, he died of heart disease at a poor farm outside Los Angeles. According to one obituary writer, "Ballin realized the hopelessness of his years of effort and told his close friends so."[31]

The time in which Ballin lived and wrote made it unlikely that his message would be noticed. Oralism and the campaign to suppress sign language continued its dominance in deaf education for forty years after his death. Perhaps this reissue of Ballin's book comes at a more propitious time. Today ASL is being taught not only to an ever-increasing number of college and university students, but also in many elementary and high schools. Sign language is probably more widely known among hearing people than at any time in history. Given that the majority of deaf students now attend local public schools rather than residential schools, Ballin's message might be even more urgently relevant today. The current solution to the dilemma of deaf education is "mainstreaming," the practice of placing deaf and hard of hearing students in classrooms with hearing children, or placing them in a special class for deaf students within a hearing school. Today, thousands of deaf students find themselves the only deaf person in their class, if not in the entire school. While they are in school, practically all of their interactions with teachers and fellow students must take place through an inter-preter—often one who is undertrained, underqualified, and under-paid.

While Ballin's idea is utopian, it is worth asking if it is *merely* utopian. Is it an entirely unreasonable goal, and would it accom-plish what he claimed for it? There have been societies in which everyone knew sign language. Nora Groce has described how on Martha's Vineyard, from the seventeenth to the nineteenth century, an unusually high rate of inherited deafness resulted in a commu-nity in which the hearing people were all bilingual in spoken En-glish and sign language. As a result, there seems to have been much less difference between the social, economic, and political lives of hearing and deaf people than is usually the case. Consonant with Ballin's vision, Groce claims a remarkable equality for deaf people on Martha's Vineyard in those years. Of course this was a small and relatively simple society. The obvious question is whether such an arrangement is likely in large, complex, heterogeneous societies such as our own, where the incidence of deafness is far lower and the likelihood for most hearing people of encountering a deaf per-son is rather low. Leaving that aside, we might also question the actual degree of equality on Martha's Vineyard. Groce reports that interpreters were used for town meetings and in church. If every-one was fluent in sign language, why did they not simply use sign language at public events and forego interpreters altogether? And why were deaf children sent off-island to attend school at the Amer-ican Asylum in Hartford?[32]

Similar questions arise with Ballin's plan, which shares with oralism problems of practicality. If few people profoundly deaf from an early age will learn to speak and lip-read sufficiently well to par-ticipate fully in the hearing world, it seems also unlikely that enough hearing people will learn sign language sufficiently well to make full participation possible. In his zeal to persuade, Ballin exag-gerates the ease with which either sign language or fingerspelling

can be learned. Could public schools ever provide a truly equal opportunity for deaf children to excel or the rich social interaction of
a school for deaf students? Ballin does not describe how his version
of mainstreaming would work. If one deaf student were present in
a class, would that class be conducted entirely in sign language?
Would the hearing students restrict themselves to sign language
whenever a deaf student was present? On what other basis would
equality be possible?

While Ballin's idea may not be "the Remedy," nevertheless, were
sign language taught in all schools with a deaf child in attendance,
it would surely mitigate the social isolation our current system in-
flicts on many. Certainly a widespread knowledge of sign language
would make our society more convenient, more welcoming, and
more accessible to deaf people in general. While it may not do
much for world peace, learning another language—in this case an
entirely different mode of communication—can do much to open
the mind, improve the intellect, and enrich one's life.

During his time in Hollywood, Ballin landed only one movie
role in which he was more than an extra. The silent film, *His Busy
Hour* (1926), was an experiment by a Hollywood director in using
an all-deaf cast. Ballin played an eccentric hermit who lives near a
high cliff by the ocean. When a rejected lover shows up to leap
from the cliff, the hermit convinces him instead to buy a suicide pill
from him. He guarantees a painless death within the hour. The
young man takes the pill and waits on the beach for death to come.
By the time an hour has passed, however, he has come to realize
that he does not really want to die. The hermit reveals that the pill
was a fake, intended to give him time to think twice about what he
was doing.[33] Like the Hermit's suicide pill, Ballin's Remedy might
not do what he promises. It probably would not by itself bring
about the full integration of deaf and hearing people on an equal
basis, nor put an end to the "clannishness" of deaf people. Ballin
thought his Remedy might be a simple solution to large and com-

plex problems, but instead it might work something like the Hermit's pill: not a solution, but an encouragement to pause and think again.

Notes

1. Preston Barr, "Albert Victor Ballin: In Memoriam," *Deaf Mutes' Journal* 61 (November 24, 1932): 1. Any unattributed quotations or references to statements by Ballin are from *The Deaf Mute Howls*. Thanks to Susan Burch for directing me to useful materials on Ballin and to Katy Stavreva for her careful reading of an earlier draft of this essay.

2. John S. Schuchman, "Oral History and Deaf Heritage: Theory and Case Studies," in *Looking Back: A Reader on the History of Deaf Communities and Their Sign Languages*, ed. Harlan Lane and Renate Fischer (Hamburg: Signum Press, 1993). While doing research on deaf people and the film industry, Schuchman interviewed an elderly woman who had had a small part in a film with Ballin, *His Busy Hour*. She remembers Ballin acting as interpreter between the deaf actors and hearing director. She told Schuchman that Ballin had good speech and lipreading skills (personal communication, February 27, 1998). In *The Deaf Mute Howls* and elsewhere, Ballin tells stories about speaking that indicate he was accustomed to communicating orally with hearing people. See also Albert Ballin, "The Life of a Lousy Extra," *Silent Worker* 40 (June 1928): 389.

3. Weston Jenkins, "Albert Ballin, Artist," *Silent Worker* 16 (January 1904): 1. See also "An Artistic Portrait," *Silent Worker* 4 (May 28, 1891): 2.

4. "Mr. Ballin Pays Us a Visit," *Silent Worker* 2 (May 23, 1889): 4; "His Hands Are Silent," *California News* 48 (December 8, 1932): 40–41.

5. *Silent Worker* 2 (June 1899): 157.

6. Quoted in Harlan Lane, *When the Mind Hears: A History of the Deaf* (New York: Random House, 1984), 371.

7. Quoted in ibid., xvi, 371. It was often noted that deaf adults almost universally opposed oralism, a claim oralists did not dispute. See Amos G. Draper, "The Attitude of the Adult Deaf towards Pure Oralism," *American Annals of the Deaf* (hereafter cited as *Annals*) 40 (January 1895): 44–54; Sarah Porter, "The Suppression of Signs by Force," *Annals* 39 (June 1894): 171; Anonymous [A Semi-Deaf Lady], "The Sign Language and the Human Right to Expression," *Annals* 53 (March 1908): 148–49.

8. James Woodward, "Historical Bases of American Sign Language," in *Understanding Language through Sign Language Research*, ed. Patricia Siple (New York: Academic Press, 1978), 333–48; Joseph D. Stedt and Donald F. Moores, "Manual Codes on English and American Sign Language: Historical Perspectives and Current Realities," in *Manual Communication: Implications for Education*, ed. Harry Borstein (Washington, D.C.: Gallaudet University Press, 1990), 1–20.

9. Woodward, "Historical Bases," 333–48.

10. Originally called the Connecticut Asylum, it was soon renamed the American Asylum, and in the 1890s took on its present name, the American School for the Deaf.

11. See Pierre Desloges, whose short book, *Observations d'un sourd et muet sur 'Un Cours elementaire d'education des sourds et muets'* (Amsterdam and Paris, 1779), is trans-

lated in Harlan Lane, ed., *The Deaf Experience: Classics in Language and Education*, trans. Franklin Philip (Cambridge: Harvard University Press, 1984), 36.

12. Nora Ellen Groce, *Everyone Here Spoke Sign Language: Hereditary Deafness on Martha's Vineyard* (Cambridge: Harvard University Press, 1985); Woodward, "Historical Bases," 333–48.

13. "Tabular Statement of Schools for the Deaf, 1897–98," *Annals* 43 (January 1898): 46–47; Jack Gannon, *Deaf Heritage: A Narrative History of Deaf America* (Washington, D.C.: National Association of the Deaf, 1981), 237–54. An excellent account of the contemporary American deaf community can be found in Carol Padden and Tom Humphries, *Deaf in America: Voices from a Culture* (Cambridge: Harvard University Press, 1988). For a concise history of the community in the nineteenth century, see John Vickrey Van Cleve and Barry Crouch, *A Place of Their Own: Creating the Deaf Community in America* (Washington, D.C.: Gallaudet University Press, 1989); see also Harlan Lane, *When the Mind Hears;* John Vickrey Van Cleve, ed., *Deaf History Unveiled: Interpretations from the New Scholarship* (Washington, D.C.: Gallaudet University Press, 1993); Renate Fischer and Harlan Lane, eds., *Looking Back: A Reader on the History of Deaf Communities and Their Sign Languages* (Hamburg: Signum, 1993).

14. Alexander Graham Bell, "Address of the President," *Association Review* 1 (October 1899): 78–79; Edward Allen Fay, "Progress of Speech-Teaching in the United States," *Annals* 60 (January 1915): 115; "Statistics of Speech Teaching in American Schools for the Deaf," *Volta Review* 22 (June 1920): 372.

15. Readers who wish a fuller exposition of the ideas sketched here may turn to my book, *Forbidden Signs: American Culture and the Campaign against Sign Language* (Chicago: University of Chicago Press, 1996).

16. Gordon W. Hewes, "Primate Communication and the Gestural Origin of Language," *Current Anthropology* 14 (February–April 1973): 5; Alf Sommerfelt, "The Origin of Language: Theories and Hypotheses," *Journal of World History* 1 (April 1954): 886–92; James H. Stam, *Inquiries into the Origin of Language: The Fate of a Question* (New York: Harper and Row, 1976); Renate Fischer, "Language of Action," in *Looking Back,* ed. Lane and Fischer, 429–55.

17. B. D. Pettingill, "The Sign-Language," *Annals* 18 (January 1873): 9; Remi Valade, "The Sign Language in Primitive Times," *Annals* 18 (January 1873): 31; Harvey P. Peet, "Notions of the Deaf and Dumb before Instruction," *Annals* 8 (October 1855): 10; J. C. Covell, "The Nobility, Dignity, and Antiquity of the Sign Language," *Proceedings of the Seventh Convention of American Instructors of the Deaf, 1870* (Indianapolis, 1870), 133–36.

18. J. C. Gordon, "Dr. Gordon's Report," *Association Review* 1 (December 1899): 206; Gardiner G. Hubbard, "Proceedings of the American [Social] Science Association," *National Deaf Mute Gazette* 2 (January 1868): 5; J. D. Kirkhuff, "Superiority of the Oral Method," *Silent Educator* 3 (January 1892): 139; Susanna E. Hull, "Do Persons Born Deaf Differ Mentally from Others Who Have the Power of Hearing?" *Annals* 22 (October 1877): 236.

19. Joseph Jastrow, "The Evolution of Language," *Science* 7 (June 18, 1886): 555–56.

20. Pettingill, "The Sign-Language," 4; Porter, "The Suppression of Signs by Force," 171; R. W. Dodds, "The Practical Benefits of Methods Compared," *Annals* 44 (February 1899): 124; John Dutton Wright, "Speech and Speech-Reading for the Deaf," *Century Magazine* (January 1897): 332–34.

21. Katherine T. Bingham, "All Along the Line," *Association Review* 2 (February

1900): 27, 29; Edward C. Rider, "The Annual Report of the Northern New York Institution for the Year Ending September 30, 1898," *Association Review* 1 (December 1899): 214–15; S. G. Davidson, "The Relation of Language to Mental Development and of Speech to Language Teaching," *Association Review* 1 (December 1899): 132; Z. F. Westervelt, "The American Vernacular Method," *Annals* 34 (July 1889): 205, 207; Gardiner G. Hubbard, "Introduction of the Articulating System for the Deaf in America," *Science* 16 (December 19, 1890): 337.

22. Letter from Alexander Graham Bell to Mary E. Bennett, August 30, 1913, Alexander Graham Bell Family Papers, Container 173, Folder-Gen. Correspondence A-C, Manuscript Collection, Library of Congress, Washington, D.C. Letter draft to the editor of the *Educator* (Philadelphia), entitled "The Question of Sign Language: Some Remarks upon Mr. Jenkins Letter," February 1894, Alexander Graham Bell Family Papers, Container 198, Manuscript Division, Library of Congress, Washington, D.C.

23. Alexander Graham Bell, *Memoir upon the Formation of a Deaf Variety of the Human Race* (Washington, D.C.: Government Printing Office, 1884).

24. A former teacher said that as a student Ballin had "small patience for routine drudgery." See Jenkins, "Albert Ballin, Artist," 1.

25. "His Hands Are Silent," 40.

26. Jenkins, "Albert Ballin, Artist," 1.

27. Albert V. Ballin, "A New York Deaf Artist at Hollywood," *Silent Worker* 38 (October 1925): 27.

28. Ballin, "The Life of a Lousy Extra," 389.

29. *Deaf-Mutes' Journal* 53 (May 4, 1924); "Deaf Mutes to Hold a Rally," Syracuse *Telegram* (October 31, 1904), clipping in Albert V. Ballin Biographical File, Gallaudet University Archives, Washington, D.C.; "Mr. Ballin's Lecture: He Tells Our Pupils about the Peculiarities of the French," *Silent Worker* 3 (February 27, 1890): 3; Jenkins, "Albert Ballin, Artist," 54.

30. On Bell, see Richard Winefield, *Never the Twain Shall Meet: Bell, Gallaudet, and the Communications Debate* (Washington, D.C.: Gallaudet University Press, 1987).

31. Howard L. Terry, "Albert V. Ballin Dead," *Deaf Mutes' Journal* 61 (November 10, 1932): 2; "His Hands are Silent," 41.

32. Groce, *Everyone Here Spoke Sign Language*, 62–63.

33. In *Hollywood Speaks: Deafness and the Film Entertainment Industry* (Urbana: University of Illinois Press, 1988), John S. Schuchman reported that he had been unable to locate any surviving copies of *His Busy Hour*. Subsequently, a daughter of one of the cast members informed him that she had a copy, which is now available on videotape in the library of Gallaudet University, Washington, D.C. See John S. Schuchman, "Oral History and Deaf Heritage: Theory and Case Studies," in *Looking Back*, ed. Lane and Fischer.

AUTHOR'S PREFACE

THIS PREFACE is an afterthought, written after many a fluttering moment of hesitation and adopted only upon my becoming convinced that a few explanations for publishing this book, as it stands, seem to be both necessary and prudent.

The original manuscript has been read and commented upon by a good many people of widely diverse tastes, and by those having more or less knowledge of the subject. While the verdict of an overwhelming majority of these readers inclines flatteringly towards its publication without changes, there arose, from the small minority, some querulous criticism upon the choice of title, harshness of certain passages, even upon my want of literary culture; (a just reproach, alas!). Some of these critics also advocated my writing the book only from a personal angle, in a gentle, wheedling subtlety, avoiding the acrid features of propaganda in order to make it wholly entertaining and secure better sales, advice of rather dubious value in this particular case. The most extensively read book, the bestseller of all, is the BIBLE, the most typical example of propaganda; certainly an excellent one to pattern mine after.

In this work I have simply put down those of my thoughts I deemed worth communicating—thoughts that have been uttered by many others—offering them in my own form; disorderly in arrangement, perhaps, but intended to lead steadily towards a single objective.

Allow me, please, to advise reading this book as a whole—**en masse,** to properly comprehend the idea, the nucleus, around which all else circles as illustration and demonstration. Segregating certain details and quarreling over them will lead nowhere.

The title appears to me to fit in with the text too neatly to be changed without emasculating the virility and force intended to be infused into the subject. It will soon be obvious to all rational minds that the deaf have been woefully miseducated, and their characters warped and stunted at their schools—terribly enough to justify the HOWL they emit. A better title or one "just as good" never occurred to my mind. None has been suggested to me as yet. Until a better one is conceived, I can see no valid reason for changing the present.

From the very beginning, it has been my earnest endeavor to set forth the facts in my possession without pausing to consider the consequences of my temerity. From certain quarters I expect some brick-bats to fly at my head. But I can anticipate them without tremor, so conscious am I that my statements are irrefutable truths. My conscience, the only tribunal I heed, leaves me tranquil over this matter.

I feel confident that by speaking the plain unvarnished truths, genuine reforms may follow in their wake. Truths are seldom pleasant to hear and I confess that I am not clever enough to know how to sugar coat the bitter pills. Perhaps I would not try to, even if I were; hence the strong reluctance I have always held against making this book entertaining, like an Arabian Nights Tales. Nevertheless, I hope that I have succeeded in making it interesting and instructive enough to hold my readers' attention from start to finish.

In reading this work you will note that I am a **deaf-mute** according to the definition I give to that term, i.e., one who became stone deaf before reaching his sixth birthday; one whose mental faculties were badly atrophied during his early childhood by total disuse of words; one who has never received any education worthy of the term at the schools built and maintained expressly for him and his kind. The wonder this book should elicit is that it could have been written at all. Is it not, therefore, rather unreasonable to expect of me a brilliant, impeccable pen?

Alterations or improvements in my language or style will not mend matters. I agree with the savant who claims that "words serve only as a beast of burden to bring ideas to the market." I shall be content if I have brought mine to you, though borne by a mangy little donkey.

The gist of my idea is that the only *remedy* for the bulk of the woes that afflict the deaf, and, for that matter, mankind in general, consists of a general use of the signs until they form **THE UNIVERSAL LANGUAGE!**

If the publication of this book should result in nothing more than making all peoples learn the manual alphabet, illustrated here, more than half of its object will have been accomplished; and this book will not have been written in vain.

Some of my friends have inquired whether the world would be willing to learn the sign language. It is not easy to answer that offhand. In my humble opinion, they will be willing in the measure that their appreciation of the idea grows. In the Middle Ages it took the people several centuries to grasp and accept as fact that the earth is globular, that it rotates on its own axis and revolves around the sun. With the progress made in communication of ideas through the press, and over the radio, we have reason to hope that a progressive idea will take root quickly in this day.

Still another purpose of this preface is to explain the presence of photographs of some of the leading figures of the Cinema. You will observe that I have been happily connected with their business, as a critic, teacher of signs, writer of studio chatter, portrait painter—even as an actor. Thus I have been afforded splendid opportunities to meet and talk on this theme with many members of this fascinating industry. Everyone was wholehearted in his or her sympathy and help. You will, I know, agree that their pictures enliven and brighten an otherwise prosaic reading. Can you resist their appeal to you to learn the manual alphabet?

I also take this opportunity to acknowledge the invaluable help I received from the celebrated naturalist, author, and artist, Mr. Ernest Thompson Seton, with whom I spent a most delightful hour, talking almost entirely in the Indian Sign Language. Moreover, he gave me permission to reprint five or six pages from his wonderful book, *Sign Talk*. I warmly recommend careful study of Mr. Seton's work, for it corroborates what I have feebly tried to put over in mine.

With diffidence in my literary prowess, but with abiding faith in the excellence of the **IDEA,** I dedicate this humble little work to the intelligent consideration of the whole world.

ALBERT BALLIN
Los Angeles, California. July 1, 1929.

Portrait of Albert Ballin

❧1❧

WHY HE HOWLS

LONG, LOUD and cantankerous is the howl raised by the deaf-mute! It has to be if he wishes to be heard and listened to. He ought to keep it up incessantly until the wrongs inflicted on him will have been righted and done away with forever.

Until today he has been a much misunderstood human being, something quite different from the rest of mankind. Even now he is shunned and isolated as a useless member of society, a pariah. His more fortunate brothers contrive to have as little to do with him as possible, and when they cannot pass him by they tolerate him from business interests, policy or unavoidable necessity, rarely from any inclination to take him to their bosoms as an intimate companion or as a close friend.

Occasionally you will come across an unusually bright, intelligent deaf-mute who awakens your interest and sympathy, but the slow, cumbersome difficulties of conversing with him stand as an unsurmountable barrier against free and equal companionship. In consequence, you drive him into seeking the society of his fellow unfortunates, for it is only among this class that he finds himself on comparative equality. When this happens you frown upon him for his peculiar "clannishness."

His misfortunes are multiplied by the unnatural methods used to thrust upon him a sort of "education," methods that stunt and warp his character by isolating him, while still young and helpless, in the institutions and schools built for him and his kind.

His peculiarities and grotesque characteristics are created by

I

you—one of the fortunates blessed with speech. They are caused by your ignorance of the real situation and by your unintentional neglect of his crying needs. You must not add **indifference** to the list of your faults—it would be unworthy of you. In the past you have been constantly deceived by his outward appearance, by sophistries handed to you by so-called experts, well-meaning but ignorant philanthropists, and by parasites who thrive and fatten on his misfortunes. You are also deceived by the quietude of the victim himself who is usually unable to present his grievances convincingly.

I realize the stupendous task I am assuming in raising as mighty an uproar as lies in the power of the very limited language at my command. This uproar has to be proportioned to the enormity of the wrong we, the deaf, suffer. Perhaps the louder, the sooner, heard the quicker our SOS may be answered.

I shall make no apologies for the unpleasant disclosures I am going to make; call it muckraking if you will, but the muck is of your own spreading, though done quite unconsciously and unintentionally. Most assuredly it is up to each of you to do your part in clearing it out. Nobody can do it single-handedly. All that lies in my power is to call your attention to its presence.

I need not, and will not try, to mince matters or gloss over the festering sores out of respect for false propriety. Neither shall I consider anyone's superficial sensibilities. In this matter I care neither for approbation nor censure. The need of the situation transcends the personal interests of any individual or group.

You may find comfort in the assurance that now there does exist a REMEDY for the sores—a reliable cure for not only the troubles of the deaf, but for others of the afflicted of mankind. Its existence is my excuse and justification for writing this book.

But for this Remedy, I would as leave think of taking up this ponderous task as flaying myself alive. Without knowledge of this Remedy, I might have accepted the present situation as an inevitable calamity for which there was no help and, like many others, rested secure and complacent in the belief that conditions were the result of an inscrutable Providence. Now I know the Remedy has been close by all the time, but its true value to humanity has never been given serious consideration.

My inquiries and reasoning on this subject led me into other byways, and in meandering through them I discovered many a new marvel promised by the universal application of this remedy—marvels that are simply dazzling in their splendor. It is such discoveries that have helped to put backbone into my zest for this often heartbreaking, thankless work. I am now convinced that the whole of society will be benefitted by this remedy.

The Remedy? What Is It?

It has been a gift of God to the Universe, to all mankind, since before Eternity. It has been used by every living being, both human and animal—perhaps by plants, too—since as far back as man can trace. It has been employed by savages everywhere, by our American Indians, to their credit, and to our discredit. The deaf vaguely appreciate its true value; they use it almost exclusively among themselves, but they seem to have overlooked its greater worth if used also by everybody else.

We all are using it to a limited extent. The only trouble is that we never thought of profiting ourselves of it thoroughly enough. We are using it only by dabs and dribbles. My proposition is that we shall, henceforth, take it in wholesale, wholesome doses.

Before proceeding with an explanation of the Remedy, let me first diagnose the ailments we are suffering from, in order to make known how best to apply with intelligence this blessed cure.

American Manual Alphabet

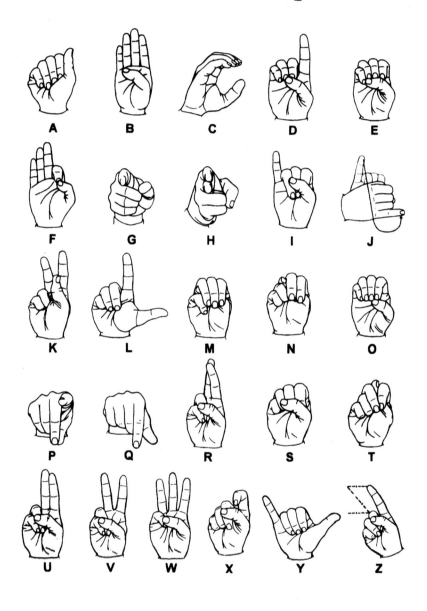

❧2❧

THE DEAF PEOPLE

DEAFNESS IS a catastrophe that smites us unexpectedly in a great variety of ways, mostly by disease and accidents after birth. About forty percent of the deaf are born so; about the same percentage are deafened by scarlet fever, the rest by meningitis, falls, catarrh, colds, brain-fever, accidents, etc., at all ages.

Fully eighty percent become deaf before reaching the age of six. Among the remaining twenty percent are a number of soldiers whose ear drums were shattered by shell shocks, discharge of great guns, and other tremendous explosions. Some scientists assert that the ever increasing volume of noises we are making threatens to make mankind a race of deaf-mutes in the not distant future.

The deaf are classified by accredited authorities and grouped under such distinctive terms as "deaf," "deaf and dumb," "deaf and speechless," "deaf-mutes," "mutes," "hard-of-hearing," etc.

For the sake of simplicity and a better understanding, I have arbitrarily divided the whole mass of deaf people into two distinct classes—**deaf-mutes** and **semi-mutes**. By the term, **deaf-mute**, I mean to designate those who were either born deaf or who became deaf **before** they reached the age of six years; and by the term, **semi-mute**, I mean those who became deaf **after** their sixth year. I wish to call strict attention to the differences between these two classes of deaf people in order to reveal the deceptions practiced on the unwary by the so-called experts, especially those who style themselves "pure oralists" and deal with the education and bringing up of **deaf children in general.**

In this country most of the deaf of school age are sent to Institutions for the Deaf, provided for and maintained at enormous expense by practically every state. Some states have several Institutions. The cost of maintaining them aggregate several million dollars annually. There are also private schools, supported by rich parents, and they are called "Pure Oral Schools," for they employ exclusively the "pure oral" method, banning altogether use of the manual alphabet and sign language. In addition there is a unique College for the Deaf in Washington, D.C., the only one of its kind in the world.[1] It is supported by the National Government.

All these schools are supposed to be giving a good education to all their pupils. But do they? I, a deaf-mute who went through the mill, can answer by relating, as briefly as possible, a few of my own experiences as a pupil at one of these institutions.

It is the practice to pass judgment on the merits of any work after it is accomplished and to care little about causes if the effects are unsatisfactory. This is especially true if the work is one with which the majority are not familiar. So difficult and intricate is the art of educating and rearing deaf children that people seldom burden themselves with a close scrutiny of methods. They leave the task to their Legislatures, their Boards of Education, and other servants whose duties are to watch over the institutions supported by the tax payers. Have these various bodies performed their duties faithfully? Most probably they, like you, are more perplexed than enlightened. I daresay that what I am going to relate will astonish, for I am, I think, one of the very few who have undertaken to speak out publicly from the angle of the victims.

The deaf are entitled to as much consideration at your hands as any other neighbor of yours. Can you, with a clear conscience, refuse to help them if you know how?

Do not surmise from the foregoing that I intend to turn your gaze solely to the dark side of the shield. I shall also show you the

---

1. Ballin is referring to Gallaudet University. *Ed.*

Painting of Rev. Thomas Gallaudet by Albert Ballin

bright side which is brilliant indeed—in a few isolated spots. One shining mark lies in the beginning of the deaf-mute's education. It has been truly beautiful, soul stirring, most promising. I cannot praise too highly the courage, foresight and devotion of the pioneers in the task of giving education to the deaf.

There are several claimants for honor and fame, but I concede the greater honor to one, Abbé de l'Épée, a French priest of the 18th Century. He is the one credited with the invention of the single-hand alphabet and the sign language still in vogue in America, a method difficult to improve upon.[2] To him should be credited the beginning of real education for the deaf. He had some brilliant disciples, the most notable one being Dr. Thomas Hopkins Gallaudet, who first introduced the system in America. But their labors were almost nipped in the bud by false priests of the pure oralism who cropped up everywhere like mushrooms—toadstools, rather. Since then real education has languished until it is now in imminent danger of complete extinction.

---

2. Ballin errs here. The one-handed fingerspelling in common use in the United States and France apparently originated in Spain before 1600. American Sign Language developed from signs used by deaf Parisians, some signs invented by l'Épée and Laurent Clerc, and signs indigenous to deaf Americans in the early 1800s. *Ed.*

❦3❧

I BECOME A PUPIL

IN PRESENTING my experiences as a pupil, I am going to attempt to make of myself a composite of all the deaf-mutes in the land, in order to average their different personalities. The school I attended will also make a composite of the many of its kind. So far as methods of educating and taking care of deaf children are concerned, there is, except in minor details, about as much difference among them as between Tweedledee and Tweedledum.

I became deaf when three years old, the aftermath of scarlet fever. Since then I have never heard voices, music or any sound— not even the firing of big guns. I have only felt, and still do, vibrations, if they reach my consciousness through other parts of the body, such as the feet and hands. This sense of sound is, of course, very faint compared with healthy ears. If the vibrations hang in the air, there remains in the atmosphere the silence of King Tut's tomb for me. If I close my eyes while standing in the midst of a crowded city street, I feel as though I were inside a subterranean cave in the desert.

My parents were people of ordinary intelligence. As may be expected, they were upset and distracted beyond expression by the calamity that befell me. They had never seen or heard of the existence of deaf people before. Through simple, crude gestures of our invention, we managed to make known to each other our wants within a pitifully limited scope. Had my family the manual alphabet, the severity of our plight might have been generally mitigated.

They could have done something to develop my mental faculties, and kept them alive and active during my early childhood.

As the situation stood they were helpless—pathetically so. Their ignorance was a blunder—a blunder worse than a crime. Owing to this lack of knowledge, they neglected the development of the nerve centers that would make me capable of understanding a spoken or written language. These nerves deteriorated and became atrophied, from disuse, as would any other part of the body under a similar condition. Others have suffered this atrophy, and I believe it to be largely responsible for the infinity of woes that cling so tenaciously to the afflicted throughout his whole life. The experiences I will present will, I am sure, bear witness to my belief. They will convince you of the absolute necessity of teaching deaf children how to read and write without delay.

As if to make reparations for their blunders, my parents did all they could to make existence smooth and pleasant for me. They left me pretty much to my own devices, deviltries, caprices; always unrestrained, unrebuked. I was splendidly cared for physically, almost spoiled by petting, but my mentality miserably neglected for four years—four tragic years. At the age of seven my mind was a clean white blank so far as written, printed or spoken language went. But it did not necessarily follow that I was stupid or feeble-minded.

To illustrate my reasoning power during childhood, let me narrate a single incident out of a multitude of others that I still remember today. The one I am about to recount happened over half a century ago.

When I was five or six, my brother, a hearing lad two years my senior, was accustomed to taking me with him to a baker's shop, a block away. After many trips to the shop I was trusted to go alone to buy and bring home a loaf of bread. My mother wrote some words on a slip of paper, wrapped it over a nickel, and put both in my little fist. She admonished me in signs to be very careful to hold fast and not to lose the coin and to bring home a loaf. I carried out the errand so satisfactorily that she patted me on the head and commissioned me to repeat a like errand a few days later. This time she wrapped the written slip over five red pennies. I always had a sweet tooth for taffy, so I stopped on the way at my favorite candy store, filched one penny, and bought a wee handful of the confection.

Then I went into the bake-shop, chewing happily. I handed the slip and the remaining four pennies to the baker. He was aware of my deafness, and he wasted no time to argue with me. He quietly scribbled something on another slip of paper and wrapped it with the bread. On my return home my mother asked me what I had done with the missing penny. I confessed my sin, and I was rewarded with a pretty stiff spanking, plus threats of a more severe punishment. I was profoundly astonished at her weird clairvoyance. How did she find me out? That set me to thinking deeply. I began dimly to suspect some connection between the baker's slip and my spanking. On my next errand I tried an experiment: I filched a penny, bought the taffy and the bread, but this time I tore and threw away the baker's nasty little slip. When I arrived home with the loaf, I watched, with a throbbing heart, to see what mama would do. She only smiled kindly and patted my head. My ruse was a grand success—my guess was right. Thereafter I stole a penny on every like errand. How delicious was that taffy!

But this mischief did not always terminate so beautifully. After the fifth round, the baker accompanied me home and spoke with mama. I must drop the curtain over the sequel. But the pain in the small of my back shot up to my head, and made it cogitate. I learned thus early that we cannot commit a sin and get away with it. Not always.

My little story may seem to be irrelevant to this thesis, but let me assure you that it is highly important. It sheds light on the big thing—that the loss of hearing does not impair the reasoning or intelligence of the victim. Unless the disease or accident that deafens the victim destroys the nerve centers, his general health does not suffer. But all communication through the ears is closed to him.

My first day of school came around at last. That horrible day. I was now to become one of the wretched inmates and waste away many beautiful days.

The Institution I went to was many a weary league from my home, an enormous, frowning edifice, housing five hundred pupils, one hundred officers, teachers, servants, etc.—a veritable army in my childish eyes.

The anguish of my parents is difficult to describe. But they sincerely believed they were doing the right thing by me. They could not do anything different.

What about my own emotions? At the tender age of seven, I was thrown into a vortex. Boys of all ages, from seven to twenty five, all gesticulating, and grimacing like apes; and I was doomed to associate on intimate terms with them for fourteen years. Oh, the nauseating homesickness I went through! It made me so ill that I had to be taken to the hospital ward for two days.

Then I was put through a strict discipline. Rules here, rules there, rules everywhere. Discipline! Discipline! Obedience!

There are those who say that discipline is necessary and good for children. I do not disagree. But I do declare that in these institutions it is carried to excess; more than half of it is an excuse to diminish burdens on the officers, and not for the education or welfare of the pupils. Unavoidable, perhaps, because of the difficulties of preserving order among deaf pupils of different mentalities and temperaments.

Small, weak, helpless, I had to submit to the inevitable. Like the other pupils, I gradually became accustomed to my new environment. Yes, I learned to like and even love their kind of life. If you keep anyone enslaved long enough, he will eventually acquire an affection for his chains. You even hear of long-term prisoners crying to be brought back to the old jail after being liberated. A similar condition is responsible for a great many deaf-mutes swearing proudly and valiantly by their "dear Alma Mater." They call this loyalty. For many years I, too, preached it.

If anyone of you have had the misfortune to be flung into an orphan asylum, you may readily imagine the life a deaf pupil leads. His character, manner of thinking, outlook on life, all are subject to pernicious influences.

And what about his education?

We are coming to that in the next chapter.

❧❧4❧❧

MY "EDUCATION" BEGINS

MY FIRST LESSON in the schoolroom was to follow the example set by my teacher in shaping my fingers to spell the letters of the alphabet. He pointed to printed letters on a chart on the wall, and explained that they corresponded with those to be shaped by my fingers.

All of this I found wonderful, and interesting. I had never before known of the existence or meaning of letters. It took me a whole week to memorize the twenty-six letters of the alphabet. We learned next to arrange and join the letters to spell the names of simple objects, such as axe, box, cat, dog, rat, etc., by comparing the words with the objects or their pictures. This occupied me during the first year. My progress was considered good, for many pupils require several years to acquire a simple vocabulary.

To appreciate the stupendous difficulty confronting me you must compare my situation with yours at the same age. Words, phrases, sentences, whole paragraphs have been dinned into your ears since birth, and you have repeated them without any great effort. You knew the meaning of many words long before you were sent to a school. All you had to learn there was how to spell and write words of which you already knew the meaning.

Before attending school, I thought only in the form of pictures or ideas—never in words. At school I had to learn to use a mind that was atrophied regarding words.

To grasp more fully the significance of my situation, try to imagine how you would begin to learn at a much later age—say at fifteen—a new language, French for instance. Perhaps you have never before heard it spoken or seen it in print. When you find it has only two genders, masculine and feminine, and no neuter, you are likely flabbergasted. Possibly you cuss when you find it difficult to make your articles in either gender and are in despair to know whether or not to pluralize things. You also struggle to make all your nouns, adjectives, pronouns, verbs, etc. agree in gender, number, tense and all else. You are confused in conjugating your verbs, especially those pesky irregulars. Likely you rage when you come to an infinity of idioms, vernacular expressions, and the endless varieties of meanings of words given to different accentuations. But you go on with dogged perseverance for ten years, and at the end you are disappointed to find yourself incapable of speaking French with the accent and fluency of a born Parisian. If, under such conditions, one was to tell you that you failed because you were **stupid,** would you not crave to push him in the face? Yet that is exactly what is said of a deaf-mute if he cannot learn his "mother tongue." The unthinking never know that there is no such thing as a **mother tongue** for a deaf-mute. They do not realize that he is learning a language more difficult by far than French would be to you. His difficulties are increased because he has to learn only through the eyes, and he has to study amidst the discouraging surroundings found only at his school.

What a blessed respite was my summer vacation and return home. But my agony as the day for my return to school approached. It was almost by force that I was brought back to the institution.

In my second term, I had to learn the difference between the singulars and plurals of the words. I recall how sincere I was in my efforts to learn, how painstaking was my teacher. He was a poorly paid man, overburdened with too large a class—about thirty boys and girls of all grades of mentality, and all as mischievous as a cage full of monkeys with sore tails.

How wildly the words danced and whirled around my head

A

while I was trying to master them—boy-boys, girl-girls, man-men (why not mans?), box-boxes, ox-oxen; incredible that the plurals for ox and box should be so different. Child-children. Did I not see somewhere on a window the sign "Childs"? Which was right? My perplexities increased. My teacher became cross. He had just succeeded in restoring some order in the class. Suddenly he confronted me, and, with menacing mien, ordered me to write on the blackboard the name of a certain domestic animal. He made gestures with his broad hands waving back and forth over his ears.

"Ass," I scrawled.

"Good. Now, what's the plural?" asked he, spreading all ten fingers.

I was stumped. He looked so fierce. What could be the plural after so many s's? After a trembling moment, I ventured the chance of adding another s to the word, making it read "Asss."

Sure enough, it brought on my head a volley of my teacher's gesticulating invectives, "Fool! Lazy! Stupid!"—ending with a resounding box on my ear.

Today I can express in words some of my emotions during childhood. I recall how I resented having my lessons hurled at me. How it seemed as if all the words, for which I never cared a tinker's damn, were invented for the sole purpose of harassing and torturing me. My punishments appeared to be for offenses that I never committed, and therefore the grossest cruelties and injustice of bad men. Oh, how I rebelled, screamed, kicked with fury. How I hated my teacher, my school, the whole creation! So wretched and homesick was I for mama that I became quite uncontrollable. For many years afterwards I was marked as one of the worst boys at school, and as such I was dealt with. I was blacklisted with regularity. I was deprived of my Saturday holidays and compelled to spend them indoors studying and committing to memory a whole chapter out of the Bible. And then to repeat it in writing, every word, without understanding one—parrot-like. That instilled into my heart a loathing for the Bible—one that has been difficult to overcome.

But what was I to do about it? I was an inmate. What could my parents do about it, even if they knew or heard of my circumstances? I could not explain to them or to anybody else. I did not know how. It must be remembered that the officers have complete control of the management of the institution and are rarely interfered with by the Board of Directors who know very little of the educational system.

Do you know the usual complexion of such Boards? Let me repeat here what I said about them in an article I wrote, long afterwards, in a magazine:

These Institutions are run by self-perpetuating Boards of Directors, composed of hearing men, with whose election the deaf have absolutely nothing to do, not one word to say. These directors owe their positions to their reputations and capacities as eminent bankers, clever real estate operators, influential politicians, and any other qualifications except as **educators** of the deaf. They meet every once in a while to hear financial reports, pass resolutions, and adopt policies, without inviting any deaf man to their councils to give them the benefit of his experiences or views in bettering the education or welfare of the deaf children. If you doubt my statement, try to "butt in," and see what's coming to you. They will, as they have in the past, ignore you with cold, silent, proud contempt. To them we, the deaf, are only stupid dummies who don't know what's good for us. Here's a pretty picture. Hopeless?

"Hopeless," I ask again? That still remains to be seen.—*The Jewish Deaf,* May, 1923.

❧ 5 ❧

I MAKE "PROGRESS"

AFTER SEVERAL years, I reached the point where it was assumed I was able to wrestle with grammar. But, consistent with my earlier childish resolution, I simply allowed words to float and swirl heedlessly around my head, making no effort to grasp them. Resolution may not be the correct term to apply to this case, for my ambition to advance myself in other directions was never quenched. Nothing was really the matter with my brain, unless we except the referred-to inexplicable atrophied centers connected with the acquirement of language. English—my mother tongue—seemed to be forever soaring miles and miles beyond reach of my comprehension. It would not or could not penetrate my head.

Nouns, adjectives, adverbs, and all their ungodly relatives gyrated and squirmed like witches on a stormy Sabbath eve to bewilder and ache my poor head. I simply sat back, looking on with a blank stare as though in a torpor, my mental eyes closed tight. I was feeling too spiritually worn out to even wish to think. These lessons were infinitely more confusing to me than conjugating irregular French verbs would be to you. You would, at least, have your English grammar at hand to help you. I had no background—nothing to guide me.

I was taught some smatterings of history, geography, arithmetic, etc., but as usual, I was too mentally atrophied to take interest in the ever-multiplying number of hard words, their complex, intricate meanings, and their innumerable secondary colors, shades, and tones. But I made marvelous progress in understanding stories when rendered in signs. They were then interesting, enthralling, though I could remember but very few names of persons, places or dates.

My teachers had, by now, abandoned trying to make me recite my lessons in writing. To them I was a hopeless case of laziness, obstinacy or sheer stupidity. They felt like the farmer who tries to make the horse drink against its will. Fagged out by the dull monotony of futile exercises in the classroom, I welcomed with delight the recesses and other dismissals from my lessons. I ran, played and forgot the little I had "learned" at school.

In our talks, we, the deaf-mutes, never communicate except by signs—only signs. It is to us the most natural, easiest and sweetest language. Spelt words are entirely tabooed among ourselves. Even persons and places are given distinctive signs of their own. The few cases where this is not practical are rare. You may be surprised to know that nearly every City, State and Country has its own sign.

Matters stood thus until the entrance of a **semi-mute** pupil into my class. It was then that something unusual transpired. But the influence he had over me must be treated separately and referred to later.

In an earlier chapter I have outlined the difference between a **deaf-mute** and a **semi-mute,** a difference as great as that of a warbling canary and a bulldog. The deaf-mute is such as I have described my composite self. The other, having become deaf when over six years old, his brain has attained a development that enables him to retain unimpaired memories of what he had heard and learned through his ears. He is much easier to teach, almost as easy as any normal child.

Many of the semi-mutes who came to my school lost their hearing at ages as late as ten, fifteen, and some when eighteen and over. Many of them had gone through schools for the hearing, some to High School, a few to College. They were the pets of the teachers and officers. In fact, they were used as **decoys** to deceive and delude the indiscriminate and gullible public.

The semi-mutes, I will repeat, number twenty percent of all the deaf. When my school had 500 pupils, it had approximately 400 deaf-mutes and 100 semi-mutes. It was always the latter 100 who were the **show pupils** at public and private exhibitions. They were the only ones shown to visitors and parents of deaf children applying for admission. The officers never explained the differences between these two classes—if such explanation could be avoided. They deliberately impressed the visitors that these **semi-mutes** were the same as **all** the other pupils, and that they owed all their education wholly to the school. No wonder then that the visitors were amazed and charmed over their mastery of English, extensive knowledge of History, Geography, and Current Events. The showing was almost as good as at any school for the hearing. Usually, what astonished the visitor was the proficiency these pupils showed in vocal speech. Their speech was plain, natural and perfect in modulation. Such visitors returned home and broadcast the glad tidings of the miracles they witnessed and lauded to the skies the "wonderful" system of instruction given to all the deaf children!

Occasionally visitors come upon a deaf-mute pupil and find him **dumb**, in all that the word dummy implies. But the institution officers are never embarrassed; they are veterans at the game, and are ready with stock explanations. The favorite ones are that these "dummies" are "exceptions," "unfortunate victims of diseases or accidents that impaired both their hearing and mental faculties at the same time." "Born that way, my dear Madam;" "vicious by nature, my dear Sir;" "stubborn in his refusal to learn;" "born idiot;" "offspring of degenerate foreigners;" "a product of the slums;" and other like deceptions that seem to fit the individual cases.

Because of this method of humbugging, the public is neither wise nor safe. The system is prolific of wrong reactions. Such an exhibition of decoys creates impressions in the minds of parents that the school can impart **articulate speech** to their deaf-mute children. Have they not seen with their own eyes, heard with their own ears, the wonderful "orally-taught" **deaf and dumb** pupils? They are definitely "sold" upon such a system of instruction.

Instead of accepting the explanation and advice of the officers who say that their children will be benefitted by the "combined method," which uses the manual alphabet and signs, the parents threaten to place their children in a school which claims ability to teach vocal speech to **all** through the pure-oral method.

Honest officers have to yield, much against their own judgment, and allow the pure-oral method to creep in, until finally it crowds out the combined system. I say they have to because otherwise the school would be closed. This pure-oral method was beginning to assume supremacy in the school of which I was a pupil. Of this method I shall speak at the proper place and time.

❦6❧

STRUGGLE WITH LANGUAGE

ONE OF THE greatest wrongs inflicted on deaf children is their enforced herding together under one roof. In these quarters they do not contact the customs, habits, or life of the normal human beings with whom they must associate after leaving school. Under the one roof, they are kept in close contact with one another day in and day out for fifteen years or longer. Like most children, they learn more from one another in five minutes than they do in a whole week from their teachers. And what do they learn? Your imagination can easily conjecture the correct answer. Most assuredly not good language or manners. In this existence, they form uncouth mannerisms, peculiarly their own—mannerisms that tend to drive them even farther apart from their future hearing neighbors.

But there are always some stray rays of brightness in the murky blackness of institutional life for the deaf-mutes. One is the presence in their midst of the semi-mutes who are helpful without realizing it. Their limited help shows the value to be gained by such contacts, for the semi-mutes are next door to the hearing.

Now I shall present as an example my personal experience upon meeting a semi-mute after I reached my fourteenth year.

At this period there came to my school, and into my class, the semi-mute alluded to in a former chapter, a boy whom I shall call Tom Wolf. He was fourteen and had become deaf the previous year. Since the age of six he had been going to a public school for the hearing. It was his great superiority in the mastery of English and general knowledge that inspired admiration, awe, and envy in us—the poor "dummies." He was one of the first to awaken my latent ability as a scholar. He and I were good friends and bitter enemies, by turns. At first he was not amiable, for he was disgusted with his new environment, believing, no doubt, that he had been cast into a crazy house. His sentiments on meeting his schoolmates were of withering scorn and disdainful contempt. He believed them to be too idiotic to learn anything in the classrooms. He did not realize until long afterwards the tremendous handicaps suffered by the deaf-mutes.

This Tom Wolf was an unusually smart chap, and he did a great deal in leading me on the right road to learning. One reason why he helped me to a betterment in manners and improvement in language was because he played upon my sensitiveness to ridicule. I preferred by far to be knocked down and pummeled than to be laughed at, and it was Tom's whim to be merciless in his laughing and sneering. Today I thank him.

But, alas, this disposition of mine was rare among the other scholars. The other pupils bitterly resented Tom Wolf's derision and air of superiority—detested him for a conceited "highbrow"—and wiped up the floor with him. In time, Tom learned to keep his mouth shut, and to cease airing his opinions of his companions' mental caliber. He had to come down a peg or two and effect a reconciliation in order to keep at peace and play with his schoolmates.

In spite of the deaf-mute's predicament as a scholar, he does try to learn, particularly when he finds himself under obligations to communicate with hearing people or to write letters to home folks. As he always thinks in pictures or ideas, he tries to marshal the few words he can muster in a manner he thinks would convey what is in his mind and the results are often very strange and grotesque. Let us examine a specimen or two:

A horse black big catch I jumped back and rided evening last yesterday.

It will be noticed that the words are arranged according to their importance in the mind of the speaker. The horse is first, its color comes next, then size, and so on to the end.

On account of his indifferent success with grammar the deaf-mute mixes his words and tenses with abandon.

I will you head strike if no stops me trouble. If you next time second you seize collar throw window out.

More expressive than elegant, but quite correct in sequence of action.

Idioms and different meanings of the same words are lost on the average deaf-mute—they slide from him like water off the back of a duck. In consequence, many an innocent, harmless situation terminates almost tragically with him. Here is a specimen:

One day, a sweet little girl received a letter from home which threw her on the floor in convulsions. She kicked and broke into uncontrollable sobbing and crying. After several futile attempts to pacify her, and to ascertain the cause, she declared (in signs) that she had unintentionally, killed her dear little brother. She pointed to the accusing line in the letter, which read: "The beautiful fountain pen you sent to Jackie **tickled him to death.**"

Another illustration, one that happened outside the school:

A fine young man (deaf-mute) was calling on his (hearing) sweetheart. She wrote on his pad, "Make yourself at home." Whereupon he went white, jumped on his feet, quaking from head to foot, hurriedly put on his hat, and rushed out of the house, resolved never to return.

A certain deaf-mute went into a stationery store to buy some writing paper. He tried to describe with his clumsy gestures the size and kind he wanted. The clerk caught on to the meaning after a while, and wrote, "Foolscap?" An awful scrimmage followed immediately.

Should the deaf-mute become entangled with the law, he finds himself in a sorry mess, for he often gives wrong answers to puzzling questions. He will say "No" when he means just the contrary. When our legal verbiage is so complicated that many hearing persons are confused, what chance has a poor deaf-mute? Recently, in Los Angeles, one was arrested and charged with a heinous breach of law. When he was examined by the police the conversation had to be carried on in writing and he committed himself in black and white with statements that incriminated him beyond reasonable doubt. He was faced with imprisonment for fourteen years. Fortunately he secured the services of a clever interpreter, the daughter of a deaf-mute couple. After questioning him for a short time she realized that he was entirely innocent of the alleged crime. Through patient, persistent explanation she convinced the judge, and the accused was set at liberty. Afterward the judge confessed he was impressed by the deaf-mute's intelligence and could not understand how such a man could blunder in answering simple questions. Incidentally, it might be mentioned that the judge was not left with a very high opinion of the institutions that are supported by the state and expected to provide an adequate education for the deaf.

In the examples I have presented I have introduced characters whose understanding of English was on a par with my own, before the advent of Tom Wolf at my school.

❧7❧

PURE ORALISM

THE PURE oralists are those so-called experts who claim that all the deaf children can be taught to articulate correctly and speak good English, **without the aid of the sign language.** It is their pet theory that the sign language is a handicap to the deaf child while at school. They point the finger of scorn at examples such as I have presented in earlier chapters and offer them as proof that the sign language makes the child think only in signs and is responsible for his neglect of English. But they forget to state that the graduates of the oral schools are, as a rule, even more deficient in English. They affect to ignore the fact that the deaf-mute child, because of his affliction, thinks from the cradle up only in pictures and ideas which, by instinct, are his most natural substitute for speech.

To you who have read closely it should now be obvious that it is not the sign language that is responsible for the poor English of the deaf-mute. His use of signs is no more to blame than is the pencil in your hand when you write.

Oralists in their efforts to suppress the use of signs practically bind the arms of the child, thereby gagging it, so it may not express itself naturally. **But even these methods can not abolish the use of the sign language.** The attempts to suppress it hinder graceful, upright growth and development, and are worse than no schooling at all. The enlightened deaf people ascribe to the methods of the oralists the uncouth, grotesque, slovenly antics and grimaces made by children reared in their schools. These children **always** invent their own signs in spite of all efforts at suppression. They are the sort that shock and prejudice the prudes against the proper and correct use of the sign language.

To be fair and just I must concede a high motive and perfect honesty of purpose to some of the oralists. But insofar as results are concerned one may as well concede the same to Tomas Torquemada of the infamous inquisition, or to the witch hunters, and to burners of heretics. So deep rooted is the prejudice against the sign language among some classes that it approaches a form of persecution.

Until his death, Alexander Graham Bell, the inventor of the telephone, headed the oralists. Because of his great fame, wealth, and his having been a teacher of the deaf in his youth, he was able to exert a powerful influence in spreading the propaganda of the oral method. As a matter of fact had Mr. Bell not invented the telephone and won fame and wealth, his views on the subject would have had no more force and weight than a goose feather in a tornado, for among eminent experienced educators of the deaf he was considered a mere tyro in this field of education.

It was Li Hung Chang, I believe, who said, "It is not what is said, but who said it that counts." This truism explains why we have so many misfits sitting in judgment and clothed with power to rule over the destinies of others.

In time the oralists, headed by the great Dr. Bell, drove the Combined System adherents to the wall. They were encouraged by the misguided parents who were crazy to hear their children prattle a few words more than just "papa" and "mama." For results, the semi-mute decoys were put on exhibition, where they posed as **orally taught** deaf and dumb pupils. At this point I must make it plain that these decoys were not aware of the use to which they were being put. They did not learn of it until long after they had left school. Then it was that they raged and fumed.

Let me proceed to explain how they teach articulation by telling a little of my own experience as an orally taught pupil, for I became one at another school in another state.

The first steps were to make me shape my mouth so, place my tongue such and such a way, and then make a sound by studying the movements of my teacher's mouth and by passing my hands over his throat or nose. If the letter "F" was to be pronounced I was made to place my upper teeth on my lower lip, and then to blow at a scrap of paper lying on the back of my hand. If the letter were a "V," I had to add a sound. The letters "M," "B," and "P" looked so much alike when formed by the lips that I was confused in knowing which of the three letters my teacher was asking me to articulate. The "R," "Ng," "X," etc. were so modestly concealed within the throat that I thought I should dive into my teacher's mouth to locate them. This entire process or method was both tedious and discouraging. I might also add that it was a bit disgusting when the teacher had partaken of onions.

You would the better appreciate the difficulties of lipreading if you were to try talking with a friend without uttering a sound; or have your friend speak aloud behind a glass partition that excludes the sound of his voice. Under these conditions try to understand his message to you by watching the play of his lips. Even with the background experience acquired by having had the use of ears and tongue in gaining an understanding of correct pronunciation and in building a vocabulary—advantages that a deaf-mute lacks—you will soon perceive the utter nonsense of educating a deaf-mute by such a method.

Some deaf-mutes do remarkably well in reading the lips. But these are the few who have devoted years and years of constant, persevering study and practice. But even they cannot understand every word spoken, unless the subject is commonplace and they are able to catch the key words and then guess the rest. To accomplish all this the individual must be prepared to neglect other branches of learning, such as History, Literature, Languages, Science, etc. Furthermore, he must come of a family who have the means to support him throughout the years. But what about the others who have to go to work for a living? Certainly the institutions supported by the state are not for the small number of prodigies who have the means to devote their life to study.

While taking my lessons in articulation, I learned that very few words in English are pronounced as they are spelt. I found that *ph* must be pronounced like *f*—laugh, laff; enough, enuff; league, leeg; and so on without number. To succeed under this condition I would have to carry a pronouncing dictionary under my arm and break off in my conversation to hunt the word and find out how it should be enunciated.

The best lip-reader requires certain well-defined conditions to read even tolerably well. The speaker must face him in a good light, at a distance of not more than fifteen feet, and move his lips broadly, slowly, and deliberately. Let the speaker turn his head sideways, talk a little too fast, or mumble carelessly, and it is good-night so far as the listener is concerned. If a speaker attempts to address an assembly of lip-readers, he may as well harangue to a blank wall. If he reads aloud out of a book it will be equally futile.

The semi-mute dislikes lipreading more than does the deaf-mute. It is no doubt the inability of the semi-mute to equal the deaf-mute as a lip-reader that is responsible for this. The reason the deaf-mute is his superior is because of his keenness of sight. This may be the operation of the law of compensation of which we often hear. But when it comes to speaking orally the semi-mute is superior to the deaf-mute. There are, of course, exceptions to this general rule—but they are few.

I met several soldiers who had been deafened by explosions. They carried pads and pencils with which to carry on conversation. They preferred this method to learning lipreading. Does this need any explanation?

If there exists any deaf-mute who has been taught orally and who can pass as a hearing person, I must say that I have never seen or read of him. If you have heard of such, I can safely bet that the odds are a thousand to one that the person is a semi-mute.

I remember how ambitious I was to learn to articulate, and my teachers thought pretty well of my abilities. My voice, I believe, was no worse than that of the average deaf-mute (at least it was not harsh enough to make a trolley car jump its tracks), but I could never learn to pronounce correctly, to modulate my voice or to make it sound natural. I cannot, even now, make my "B" sound different from "P," my "D" differ from "T," and my "R" is always missing. Because of these deficiencies I often make queer blunders that either amuse or disgust my hearers. Let me relate an incident or two to illustrate the "brilliant" results of my education in articulation.

I made a social call on a lady friend while she was giving a tea party to a large circle of acquaintances. She was on the point of sending her maid to make some purchases when it occurred to me that I wanted a package of cigarettes. I asked her if I could have the maid bring me a box of a brand then in vogue called "Duke's Best." I spoke vocally. To my astonishment the whole company broke out laughing. Upon my request to be enlightened, she reluctantly told me that I pronounced my request like this: "Pleeze keet me a-ah pox of dogs pest."

At another time and place I tried vocally to deliver my holiday greetings: "I wish you a Merry Christmas." In spite of my efforts, the sentence sounded like: "Eye wisch yeo-u a-ah Mary kiss my—."

My mistakes, deplorable though they were, were mild and innocuous compared to those made by others—some of which are downright obscene, though not so intended by the speaker. Under such conditions can you imagine how women feel about it when they learn how such blunders have changed the meaning of their speech. You can appreciate why they would blush with mortification, and disappear. After such experiences no amount of entreaty, persuasion or threats can persuade them to again open their mouths to utter another word in public this side of eternity. All their long years of toil in school, all their sacrifices of subjects more worth while than oral speech and lipreading, are for nothing.

I could go on interminably citing other examples of the disastrous results of the present system of "education"; but I will bring this chapter to a close with one more tale—one that is almost unthinkable.

For the moment I shall stuff your ears with wax so you cannot hear a sound, and I shall ask you to imagine yourself a deaf-mute, my pupil, whom I am teaching by the oral method. I must also ask that you imagine you have never heard music before. Now I take you into a room where for the first time you see a Paderewski seated before a piano, playing one of the classics. I command you to watch **sharply.** Next I urge you to lay your hands on the piano to **feel** the vibrations. You obey me because I am your master, ready to reward or punish you. I insist that your eyes must become your ears. My deepest regret is that I cannot help you to smell the music. You watch the pianist move his hands gracefully across the keyboard and watch his nimble fingers as they strike the keys. He brings his hands down with a thundering crash. Then his fingers and hands barely move as he comes to an andante passage. His body seems to swing and sway rhythmically. After this performance I make you sit before the piano and order you to reproduce the same composition as accurately, and with the same musical taste as he rendered it. You will fail at first. But you must not become discouraged. Brace up, and try it again. You will win out at the end of fifteen, twenty-five, or maybe a thousand years. **It will be your own fault if you fail!**

This you say is ridiculous. Oh, no! No more ridiculous than the extravagant claims made by some of the oralists as to their ability to teach the deaf children any and all things, and so well that they will be fully restored to the society of hearing people.

8

THE GRADUATE

TODAY THE deaf-mute graduates and goes into the world poorly equipped and prepared for the task of taking care of himself. During his life at school, every one of his actions has been regulated by rules designed more for the benefit of his teachers than for himself. He has so long been denied the right to think for himself that he is now an automaton with no initiative of his own. He is conscious that in leaving school he is "free," but he does not know what to do with his freedom. He is dazed. He feels like the long-term prisoner or slave suddenly liberated from captivity. With the habit of child-like dependence upon others bred into his soul, he seeks sympathy and help from his fellow unfortunates. Usually he is guided to the parsonage of some Church for the Deaf, where the parson is a deaf man with a sympathetic understanding of his kind. After looking into the case with care, this good parson tries to find employment for the graduate, a heart-breaking task, because of the deep-rooted prejudice against employing deaf-mutes. Unless the graduate is more skillful than the average hearing man doing the same kind of work, it goes pretty hard with him.

The school he just left teaches several trades, such as tailoring, baking, printing, cabinetmaking, carpentry, shoemaking, and a few others; but the methods taught are all so antiquated that the pupils are seldom able to handle modern tools or machines. The schools cannot be blamed for this, for industry is constantly introducing new machinery and methods, and the schools have not the finances to follow suit. The one I attended had a large printing equipment. It was set up over sixty years ago, and has been changed but slightly since then. The graduate from that shop had to begin as a "printer's devil" and learn all over again.

But a small percentage of the graduates follow the trades they learned at school. The majority, unless they have well-to-do relatives to help them, are half-starved before they become proficient at a trade that does not call for the use of the English language.

A few deaf-mutes possess talent for highly skilled work like Commercial Art, Carving in wood, clay or marble, Architectural Draughting, Decorative Painting, and Illustrating. This is found even among the most illiterate. But the poor devil is up against it good and plenty if he is ignorant of English while working at one of these arts. Sometimes he is employed on trial. He receives in writing instructions as to what he is to do. Often he cannot understand them. If he turns to his fellow workers for explanation, he finds that none of them know the sign language, and therefore cannot help him. He scratches his head, makes wild guesses, and goes ahead, taking desperate chances. He makes mistakes. The boss tears his hair and kicks him out, vowing never again to employ another "dummy." This poor "dummy" then has to give up his cherished vocation and wash dishes, help the janitor, scrub floors, or undertake some other form of menial labor.

Is it not a pity that he did not find a boss who could understand the sign language? If he had, both might prospered together happily. But, alas, such employers are as scarce as hens' teeth.

There are, today, many graduates from Gallaudet College working side by side at manual labor with deaf-mutes from Russia, Poland, Germany, Italy, and other countries who can scarcely scrawl their own names. They grumble at their lot, and ask, with wonder, what is the use of higher education, if all it fits one for is making bed springs, auto tires, etc. Often the foreigner draws higher wages. Many of them never went to any school, but they did receive thor-

Betty Compson was the model for this Albert Ballin painting,
A Hawaiian Idyl.

ough training at some trade like tailoring, cutting garments, carving, engraving on copper, stone or steel, and similar trades that require extraordinary dexterity.

There are rare cases where genius, by sheer force of ambition, pride or unusual opportunities, overcomes all handicaps and rises in spite of, not because of, institutional life and training. It is also strange that most of the artists among the deaf are found in Europe, where schools for their kind are few and considered inferior to those in this country.

The deaf-mute does not wish to be an object for compassion. He craves neither pity, nor charity. Should you be approached by anyone extending his hand to you for alms on account of his deafness, it is high time for you to yell for the police, for the chances are ninety-nine out of one hundred that the panhandler is an imposter. The deaf-mute has pride and believes himself as good as any man alive. All he asks for, nay, **demands,** as his birthright, is to be respected and treated as an equal and be given an equal chance in this life. He does not want to be discriminated against because of his impediment.

9

ALEXANDER GRAHAM BELL

I WAS FORTUNATE in having had for my father an artist—a lithographer to be exact. He took me out of school when I was sixteen, which is five years earlier than is usually allotted to a pupil for graduation. I am certain it was this step that saved me from becoming a confirmed dummy, because the older one grows, the harder it is for him to change acquired habits. But my father did not take me from school because he mistrusted the system. He simply decided that I could not begin any too soon to learn drawing and painting, for he desired me to become a painter of pictures. He put me in the studio of an Italian artist and also had me attend Cooper's Union in New York. A year later, I entered the studio of the great H. Humphrey Moore.

To me it was indeed a strange world. I could not have felt more different if I had been magically transported to another planet. After some intimate association with hearing people, mostly art students, I began to perceive that I was different from them in endless ways. At first I was positive I was right, and they dead wrong. I was stubborn in adhering to the odd ways of thinking and acting that I had acquired while at school. I wondered, with a sinking heart, why I was shunned and left severely alone. I had to go through much pondering before I realized it was I who was at fault—that I was a thorough going dummy in my habits, behavior, ideas, language, character, outlook on life—all of which made me repulsive to my new acquaintances.

It was the perseverance of my family, who had by this time

36

learned enough of the manual alphabet to talk with me, that helped me to mend my ways. But it proved a slow process, for I had to unlearn what I had been taught and acquired at school, and it is human nature for one to cling tenaciously to early acquired prejudices and habits. Frankly, I rejoice that I left school while very young, while my mind was still flexible enough to absorb new and better influences. The known effect of childhood impressions on later life should convince the serious minded of the need of the right schooling for the deaf.

As I manifested signs of talent in my art work, some rich relatives sent me to Europe for intensive study. There I lived for three full years without meeting a single deaf-mute. I did not purposely avoid them. I merely did not seek them out; and I never missed their company.

On the third day after my arrival in Paris, I was sauntering along the beautiful Avenue des Champs-Elysees. My eye caught the sign "Restaurant Ledoyen." Without further ado I strolled inside. With cheerful nonchalance I ordered a sumptuous repast, including a full quart bottle of heady old wine.

As was to be expected, the fumes went to my head, and all objects around me swam and floated giddily. Finally I gesticulated to my waiter to make out my bill. My gestures attracted the attention of a fine looking, portly, black-bearded man sitting at a table just behind mine. He beckoned my waiter and asked him if I were a deaf-mute. Upon receiving the latter's affirmative nod, he walked over and seated himself at my table. At first he spoke orally. I shook my head, and pointed to my ear—the sign a deaf man usually makes to indicate his impediment.

"Parlez-vous francais?" spelt he on his fingers.

I again shook my head.

"Are you English?"

I shook my head emphatically, and spelled on my fingers, "I'm an American!"

"So am I." He laughed and shook my hand. Then, he gave me

Dreaming, painted by Albert Ballin

his card. I could not read the fine print, it was too blurred by the alcoholic fumes in my head. I nodded gravely as if I understood and put it in my vest pocket. Then I handed him my card.

After some desultory conversation through which I fumbled foolishly, I begged his pardon for my appearance, remarking that I was not accustomed to European climate.

"Yes, I can see that plainly enough," he laughed.

I tried to rise, but my legs wobbled, and I sank helplessly back into my chair. I had to ask him to kindly pay my bill, handing him my pocketbook, saying, "I can't make out these silly pale blue French bank notes!"

He courteously complied with my request. Moreover, he ordered a fiacre, and took me to my hotel. Thereafter all was a blank until I recovered consciousness next morning and found myself in my hotel room, suffering from a ringing headache. I recalled the meeting with a fellow countryman and jumping out of bed I sought his card. It read "Alexander Graham Bell."

Oh, oh!

The next day I received a note from him, inviting me to join him at dinner at his hotel.

"Are you acclimated?" were his words of greeting upon my arrival. What a jolly host he was. What a glorious evening I spent with him. Afterward he was fond of recounting to others the ludicrous manner by which we met. I usually countered by twitting him over the use of sign language, which he affected to detest, but which was responsible for bringing us together.

I saw him several times while in Paris; we parted company when I moved on to Rome. But within the month he was in Rome and we met again—and several times thereafter. He was, I learned, on the point of setting out for Egypt with his family, consisting of his lovely wife who was as deaf as I, two sweet daughters (one of three years and the other five), their maids, governesses, private secretary, valets de place, valets de chambre, guides, footmen, etc. (mostly the etc.). Included in the party was his venerable father

Melville Bell, who had prepared charts, with diagrams of the tongue, lips, throat, nose and other organs of speech. His object was to describe their positions in speech and thereby assist in teaching articulation to deaf children. The party was later increased by the arrival of Col. J. Gardiner Hubbard, Dr. Bell's father-in-law, and his own retinue. What an immense company. I asked the doctor if he were aware how much the jaunt to Egypt would cost him. He acted as if he were alarmed, and asked me how much it would. I exclaimed, "Why, it can't be less than $10 a day for each person." I counted fifteen in his party alone and added, "Oh, fully $150." He pretended to be dismayed and turned to consult his secretary for a few minutes, after which he assured me, "He (meaning the secretary) tells me that we are getting about $100,000 a month. I guess we can stand the racket." I was so dumbfounded that I blurted out, "If that's true, you can certainly include me in your party!"

"Sure," he answered, "Come along if you like!"

But that trip was never undertaken, for shortly afterwards both his daughters were stricken with scarlet fever, and they were very ill indeed. In fact they nearly lost their hearing. This illness detained the family in Rome for three months. When the children recovered, it was then too late in the season to continue to Egypt. They turned north towards Nice and from there on home to America.

Their stay in Rome afforded me opportunities to become more intimate with the doctor. He was always busy, trying to invent something else. He had, at the moment, a bulky mass of machinery or apparatus. He said that he was trying to produce sound by light.

"To make the deaf hear by light?" I facetiously inquired.

"No, no! I don't know yet to what purpose it may be put, if successful. All great inventions are like children, we never can tell what they will turn out to be until they are grown."

His favorite hours of labor were during the night from 8:30 to 4 a.m. "Until five or six when my wife is not looking on," he used to say with a merry wink.

I should record now that there never existed a more gracious, more affable, more fun-loving or jollier fellow on this sorry old globe than Dr. Bell. His character was without blemish. Still, it does not necessarily follow that his ideas or judgment on all things was infallible. In criticizing his theories on the education of the deaf, I have not the slightest intention to impute insincerity on his part. He was absolutely honest in his beliefs. But his beliefs were, in my opinion, and the opinion of many others, altogether wrong. His love and sympathy for the deaf were boundless, and should never be questioned. He spent a considerable part of his wealth and time on his favorite theory concerning the deaf. It was his hobby. Still, his expenditures and energies were, I believe, sadly misspent. In fact they have brought misery to the ones he loved and wanted most to help.

Though a confirmed pure oralist, Dr. Bell was a fluent talker on his fingers—as good as any deaf-mute—and could use his fingers and arms with bewitching grace and ease. His wife was charming, beautiful and intelligent. Though a deaf-mute in the sense I have defined, she was a comparatively fine lip-reader. But it is with regret that I cannot say one word in praise of her articulation. Even today I find it difficult to convince others that she could not spell on her fingers or make signs. I never saw her do either. In conversing with her, I moved my mouth without making any sound, and she always answered in writing, an anomaly of social intercourse between two deaf-mutes. She understood every word I spoke, if I moved my mouth broadly, deliberately, and if the topics were commonplace. One evening I begged Dr. Bell to spell orally one word, to see if she could catch it. I selected **Fujiyama** (the holy mountain of Japan). He rebelled, explaining that that word was foreign. But finally he yielded to my entreaty. He took her on his lap, and pronounced each letter slowly and repeatedly, "F. ef, not ve, just fu, fu—eye, ah ah—ama." It took him some minutes, but she later succeeded in spelling the whole word correctly in writing.

He turned around to me with a triumphant light in his eyes and smiled as though to say, "Now you see!"

41

THE DEAF MUTE HOWLS

I shrugged and spelt on my fingers, "Why waste minutes, when spelling the word on the fingers will take but seconds?" He also shrugged, and waved aside my sly thrust as inconsequential. Then began a heated argument:

"That is a mere persiflage in contradiction of the psychoanalysis and final diagnosis of the vertical parallelogram on the reasoning, as differentiated from the horizontal—and—."

These are not his exact words, but to me they sounded equally intricate and involved. Perhaps you too, have encountered some learned pedagogue who obscured his arguments with unintelligible, scientific jargon. Like myself, you were probably ashamed of your ignorance, and of your inability to pay back in like coin. Therefore you assumed an air of wisdom and answered, "You are right—perfectly right, my dear Sir. I understand perfectly." Then glancing at your watch you added, "But please excuse me. I've an important engagement. Good night!" And then you scooted.

I "scooted" that night. I was so young and inexperienced—twenty—that I could not possibly answer such a torrent of eloquence. But in my heart I was not at all convinced by his argument. Then and there I resolved not to again hurt his feelings and bring upon my head another avalanche of jaw-breaking words.

At other times Dr. Bell regaled me with stories. He was a regular chatterbox, but intensely interesting. Some of his stories have a pertinent bearing on my theme, and I am saving them for the following chapter.

꧁10꧂

DR. BELL'S STORIES

ONE UNFORGETTABLE night, Dr. Bell and I ensconced ourselves in a cozy corner at his hotel, and we talked from eight in the evening to four in the morning. We touched on a great variety of subjects. To be exact I should say it was he who did the talking, and I the listening. He was a fascinating raconteur. When in good humor—and he usually was—he used no heavy, scientific phraseology to overawe me, and in consequence I never noticed the flight of time.

He bared to me the intimate things of his life. He was at one time a teacher of deaf children at Boston, Massachusetts, at a salary of six hundred a year. His wife, before her marriage, was one of his pupils. He employed, of course, the oral method exclusively, for to him it was the one and only method. He claimed that, in teaching the sign language to deaf children, we give them a language which no one else uses, and encourage the deaf to **refuse** to learn English. It is now clear to me that the doctor was never conscious that he was reasoning from an entirely wrong premise—putting the cart before the horse. I did not then know anything about the subject, so I could not argue with Dr. Bell.

Often, he wandered from this subject of the deaf, and talked of how, by an accident, he invented the telephone. His wife, while still his pupil, called his attention to a curiosity. She told him of feeling vibrations of sound on her muff while in the streets. It set him to experimenting with various devices, seeking always to use them to help the deaf hear. In due course of time, he developed and made the **telephone.**

He described, in his droll way, how he tried to raise funds to exploit the patent. He offered to sell a half interest to a neighbor for $1,000. But the neighbor guffawed and exclaimed, "What! Me throw away one thousand good bucks on a scientific toy? Nothing doing!" Today, not even Henry Ford is rich enough to buy that half interest.

He told me a number of other interesting anecdotes, but as they have nothing to do with the theme, I have to (most regretfully) omit them.

On one occasion, after a long period of silent meditation, he blurted out an exclamation that **"all the schools for the deaf, both the combined and pure-oral, should be razed to the ground!"** This explosion caused me to prick up my ears. (One of the first and only occasions upon which I could use them for any purpose except as ornaments.) He explained that the herding together of the deaf children under one roof cruelly hurt the poor things. Then he proceeded to talk on some of the evils already touched upon in this book. This brilliant flash of truth remained with me—although I did not realize its full significance then. Now that I have come to a realization, may I be pardoned for throwing my cap in the air and shouting, "Three Cheers for the Razing!"

As well as my memory will allow, I shall explain how the doctor hoped to improve the methods of education:

Deaf children [he said] should attend public schools for the hearing, where they may play and study on equal terms with children who hear. Teachers, specially trained, should be engaged to keep their progress abreast of the others. The children could then live with their own folks, and have all the benefits of home life and influences. In short, they would live the normal life of the hearing.

I asked him how he would take care of the children who live apart from the schools where the special teachers work. He dismissed my objections with the statement that in the country districts the children could be housed in cottages in small groups, where a special teacher and his wife would give them the same home influences and care as they would their own children. He stressed the need of the deaf children being kept far apart from their kind to eliminate the faults peculiar to the deaf. He presented more details, but they were couched in scientific terms and now escape my memory. To me, the most impressive feature of his discourse was his championing of the pure-oral method. Having left my school but four years before meeting Dr. Bell, I knew from practical experience that the method he favored was not practical.

After the doctor's departure from Rome, I did not see him again for three years. We met in New York, and later at his home in Washington, D.C., where I was always certain of a warm welcome.

True to his belief, the doctor continued working to spread the gospel of the oral method. Either because he was appalled by the enormous difficulties of putting into effect his idea of razing the existing institutions, or because he had conceived a more feasible plan, he never again referred to the razing. Perhaps he felt that the "Day Schools," springing up everywhere, met the need, for they are now superseding the old institutions and their antiquated methods.

He continued to be prodigal in time and money in order to fasten on us the oral method. He founded the **Volta Bureau** to further spread his propaganda. Next, he hired "educators" to tour the country and to persuade Legislatures and heads of the old schools to introduce and enforce its exclusive use. He even brought before Congress a motion to prohibit, by legislation, marriages among the deaf to prevent increase of congenitally deaf children.[1] Fortunately, his arguments on this matter were deemed unsound, and it failed to pass.

But, to my sorrow, he succeeded only too well in establishing his cherished oralism at all the Day Schools, and the majority of

---

1. This story is widely believed. Bell opposed marriages between persons born deaf, but he did not support laws prohibiting such unions. *Ed.*

the old institutions. He had, for his opponents, many experienced educators who fought valiantly but in vain.

The Day Schools were built expressly to permit children to remain with their families, and benefit by home influences and association with the hearing. But this plan has failed miserably, because of two insurmountable obstacles: One is that no deaf-mute child can be taught orally to make himself intelligible to his hearing companions; and **the other is that the hearing children are never taught to talk on their fingers or to make signs. THIS IS THE GREATEST MISTAKE OF ALL.** The gulf between the deaf and the hearing is as wide and deep as ever—and there has appeared no way of bridging it. The deaf pupils of the Day Schools do not, and cannot, meet and play with the hearing. When they leave school they are drawn to the society of their own kind, and the purpose for which the Day School was created meets defeat.

In concluding my little stories of Dr. Bell, allow me to repeat once more that, as an individual, he was a prince of good fellows, and intended to be a friend of the deaf. His idea of razing all the institutions for the deaf, including the ridiculous Day Schools, was most excellent. This razing ought to begin in earnest. Later in this little volume, I intend showing how it can be done easily and cheaply.

Dr. Bell's fame as the inventor of the telephone will live forever—his greatest monument—glory enough to satisfy the most ambitious. His mistakes in the educational field may be excused. It has never been allotted to any one man to know everything. May the soul of this great man rest in peace.

⚡11⚡

STILL AN INFERIOR

JUST A FEW words more about my life in Italy—three years that were fruitful in experiences and made interesting because of my study of other worthwhile subjects.

Without intent to avoid meeting with deaf people, I met none during my entire sojourn in Italy. I neither missed nor craved their company for the simple reason that Italy is, **par excellence, THE LAND OF GESTURES!** My memories of my life while there will remain pleasant the rest of my days. I earnestly recommend Italy to all the deaf as the country where they can feel completely at home, and live on equality with the hearing without knowing one word of spoken or written language. The Italian will preserve and use his peculiar but expressive sign language to make himself understood. On the day following my arrival in Rome, I became a member of the Circolo Artistico Internazionale, a club composed of about 400 painters, sculptors, singers, musicians, authors and members of the Nobility. It was most democratic. All it demands of its members is that they contribute something to advance Art, Music, Drama, Literature—in brief, the cultural arts.

With the warm sympathy of the Latin race, these people were most cordial, and succeeded in making me very happy. I did not know one word of Italian, but that never bothered me. My new friends—delightful fellows—made gestures so simple and complete that I missed not the smallest shade of meaning in the complete stories with which they regaled me the first evening. Long afterwards, I repeated these stories in the same manner to my deaf friends, and they relished them as keenly as I did. My wish is that I could reproduce them, but as they were rendered in signs, it cannot be done. To obtain some clear idea of what they were like, imagine yourself in a theater watching the gestures of the inimitable Charlie Chaplin, who can tell entire stories without uttering one word.

The French and Greeks make simple signs that vary slightly from the Italians; but are just as easy to learn. All gestures are, however, limited in scope, being intended to emphasize vocal expressions, and not as a language. The sign language, as used, is neither elegant nor artistic. It has never been cultivated or developed as a distinct means of expression, unless we except the few, isolated, dilettante cults like the Delsarte Schools of expression which give lessons in pantomime to actors and pantomimists. In the Combined System Schools for the Deaf, it is used by the teachers to explain the meaning of words to their pupils. The deaf people use it in a **conversational style** and each individual fits it to his taste without caring whether his gestures are graceful or ugly. He is satisfied with making himself understood with little effort—a habit that retards progress toward beauty and poetry in the use of signs. Such is the status of the sign language today. Quite different from what it was in the days of the pioneers in the education of the deaf-mutes— before the advent of pure oralism. Now the number who can truly employ the sign language effectively can be counted on the fingers of one hand. Unless the art be taken up and cultivated, it runs the danger of becoming as extinct as the fabled dodo.

On my return to America, I found myself once more among stiff-necked people whose few gestures are cold and meaningless. It reminded me again that I was indeed a **deaf-mute**—helpless and useless, an outcast in society. It would be still worse had I, like a large majority of deaf-mutes, been unable to write. Many times I longed to return to sunny Italy! Now when I wish to converse, I have to resort to the slow, cumbersome, process of writing—the only safe, sure medium of the deaf. Then there is always the chance that the third or fifth person I meet cannot read or write at all. This

Neil Hamilton (left) learning to fingerspell his own name,
with Albert Ballin's help.

is an angle that I shall discuss later. Now when I converse, I have to write my conversation, and the one with whom I am conversing has to be patient while I labor with pencil and paper. Then I in turn have to wait while he writes an answer. Again and again we dash off notes. While waiting for me to write, my acquaintance likely swears at me for not having learned to talk with my tongue and read his lips. **His time is valuable to him.** While I mentally anathematize him for not having learned the manual alphabet and signs. **My time is valuable to me.** Outwardly, both of us are all smiles and sweetness. He tolerates me for a reason; while I, too, have reason to cultivate him. We part with suppressed oaths, and a determination to dodge each other in the future.

Whose fault is it—his or mine?

It may now look like fifty-fifty to you. But I hope you will look at it differently **after** you have finished this book.

❦12❧

THE UNBRIDGED GULF

A GREAT MANY of the deaf are employed at manual labor side by side with hearing co-workers. Throughout the day they must limit conversation to matters pertaining to the work at hand. At the close of the day, each seeks the company of his own kind. At their clubs, fraternities, etc. congregate all classes of the deaf and hard-of-hearing. No matter how they may differ in tastes, mentality, race or religion, they are thrown together. When differences arise, to the point that they become intolerable, certain factions break camp, and form other clubs. But the new ones are always of the same sort, composed of all species, and, as always, shut away from the mass of humanity that hears. The deep, wide gulf between the deaf and hearing remains unbridged.

The enforced herding inherited from school life gives rise to the erroneous belief that the deaf are, **by nature,** clannish, narrow, and class-conscious. All they need is a bridge—a means of conversation—to connect them with those that hear. **Then the deaf as a CLASS will disappear altogether and forever.**

I propose to present a picture of this bridge, a bridge of wonderful solidarity, guaranteed to last. The material to build it abounds on every side; it is evident at all times. To see it without giving it notice or appreciating its true value, we are as blind as when we saw steam without realizing its power until one John Watt showed us how it could benefit mankind.[1] How many millions of men had

---

1. Presumably, Ballin means James Watt, inventor of the steam engine. *Ed.*

seen quadrillions of apples fall from trees before an Isaac Newton saw one—and thought about it for the first time? Did not his thinking result in an understanding of a fixed law?

Of what material is my bridge? Nothing more or less than the sign language, although still in the rough, unhewn and unpolished, as the deaf have used it. Now we should think about making it attractive. Remember that the American Indians use it among themselves and in their contacts with other tribes as a distinct language. They employ it in a form that is more dignified than the form of the deaf. But it is still lacking in artistry and limited in range. In a preceding chapter I have explained how it is used as emphasis in oral speech among the southern races, such as Italians, Greeks, French, etc. As one travels north, the use of signs and gestures lessens, until we find only traces among the English and inhabitants of colder climes. Perhaps the latter feel the cold too keenly to wish to take their hands out of their pockets.

The instinct to use gestures has never been completely suppressed anywhere on the earth. It explains why deaf children take to signs and gestures as naturally and zealously as ducks to water when they find other mediums of self-expression beyond them.

It is a fact that hearing children learn the sign language more readily than do adults. I have met some learned college professors who wrestled with it for months, but in vain. What is the reason?

My wife had four congenitally deaf brothers and sisters and therefore became accustomed to using signs from infancy. Naturally she was as proficient as they. Indeed, she can, when the whim seizes her, pass for a deaf-mute.

Our firstborn surprised us by making signs for milk or water when only nine months old—long before she could stand or prattle one word. Our second child performed the same feat. We flattered ourselves that we had prodigies for offsprings and bragged to our married deaf friends. But they only laughed and demonstrated that their children acted the same, and at an earlier age than our children. Further investigations revealed the fact that hearing children of deaf parents **always** excel in the elegance and brilliance of expression in signs. Furthermore, as normal children, blessed with all the five senses, they easily forge ahead, because they get a real education, and pass through many experiences and emotions that the deaf don't. As these truths, and a few others yet to be touched upon, grew clearer, I arrived at the conclusion that it was so easy to teach and to learn the sign language that there was no longer any valid reason why it should not be taken up by all. It should be self-evident to everyone that not only the deaf, but they themselves, and the whole world would benefit by such a step.

It now remains to discover the Master Mind capable of planning and constructing this magnificent bridge. When it is completed, it should be called the "Bridge of Signs."

❧13❧

KINDLING THE IDEA

THE IDEA of the Universal Sign Language as the bridge dawned on me slowly. While it was still but a shadowy vision, I discussed its possibilities with some of the brightest of my fellow deaf. It dazzled a few, but to others it did not appear surprising. Some scoffed at it as too Utopian. They reminded me how they had tried to interest the public through conventions, addresses to Legislatures, publications, and distribution of manual alphabet cards, but all to no avail. They had not created the tiniest ripple on the stagnant waters of the sea of ignorance and indifference. A few had petitioned the Legislatures in certain states to order the placing of at least one page of the manual alphabet in the textbooks used in the public schools. But they were turned down. Why? One reason advanced was the fear it inspired that it might encourage whispering among the scholars. My, oh, my! This attitude is similar to refusing to build a magnificent skyscraper for fear that it might house a vagrant little mouse. At times the intellect of some of our legislators is beyond understanding.

These many objections may seem strong enough to dampen hope and ardor, but the idea is too strong to die. In my judgment, the deaf have erred in the methods they have employed. Their appeal to legislative bodies may be likened to the chirping of a lone sparrow. What is needed are more vigorous methods that will reach the ear of the public and awaken them to the needs of the deaf. I hold tenaciously to my faith that the idea which I am presenting will eventually blaze forth. Meanwhile I can lie low like "Bre'r Rabbit" and practice patience.

Some years ago I contacted an unusually smart chap, J. Parker Read, Jr. He was to solicit advertising for a novel form of perpetual calendar which I had invented and patented. He was able to learn the manual alphabet in exactly five minutes, and enough of the sign language for practical purposes in three days. The average length of time required is one hour for the manual alphabet and one month for the number of signs he acquired in three days.

It is so easy to learn the manual alphabet that I have made it a rule for my acquaintances among the hearing to learn it if they intend to become my friends. This is my test of their sincerity. The rule, however, is not original with me. Many others among the deaf made it theirs long before. I know of a photographer in New York who lost his hearing when eighteen.[1] He has won prominence in his profession, and he demands that his many employees learn the manual alphabet if they wish to hold their positions. Incidentally, this gentleman is now past sixty and can talk so well orally that he is often mistaken for a hearing man, but, like most semi-mutes, he is a failure as a lip-reader.

Mr. Read, of whom I have spoken, was indeed a hustler. He found time while seeking advertising contracts to study the mysteries of motion-picture production which, at that time, was coming into prominence. This new form of entertainment appealed as strongly to me as it did to Read. I began to dream of its possibilities in elevating civilization and bringing about a universal brotherhood of man. It was then an entirely new form of sign language—the one, in my opinion, destined to become universal. While still crude, it was advancing by leaps and bounds. Its poor relative, the language of the deaf, lagged behind. But screen pantomime did make the public realize what could be expressed without the spoken

---

1. Ballin probably is referring to Alexander L. Pach. *Ed.*

55

Albert Ballin teaching Laura La Plante to fingerspell.

word. Now that the screen talks it has lost its world appeal and is limited.

Mr. Read's enthusiasm helped in sending him to Cuba, where he filmed the raising and final burial of the USS *Maine*. When he returned he told me of adventures that were, indeed, thrilling. Later, his boundless energy drew him into bigger ventures. I could do nothing but look on helplessly, and feel depressed because of the handicap that prevented my participating. To become an actor, director, or anything, it seemed imperative to be able to hear and to speak orally.

Here, the dummy need not apply.

Shortly afterwards, Read was called to California, and I lost sight of him for a few years. In the meantime, the Great War and Prohibition came thundering along, wrecking my little business by putting out of commission most of the hotels and cafes where my calendars were installed. It was fortunate for me that during those troublesome days I found a position as companion to a deaf, dumb and blind boy at a seashore resort, not far from New York. This boy reminded me of Helen Keller, who is known for her remarkable accomplishments and high intellectual attainments. But the boy was not her equal in mental stature. He was, however, gifted with a marvelously retentive memory. He could recognize people once introduced to him by the feel of their hands. Once told, he never forgot the birthday of a friend. These and other details that readily escape the memory of most of us were always at his command. He could solve difficult chess problems, and move the pieces about on the board. On one occasion I tested him by asking him to commit to memory some difficult French words and to act as my memorandum book.

"What is French for Cannibal?" I suddenly fired at him. Without pausing for an instant he shot back, "Anthropophage."

Although I have not seen this boy for many years, I am willing to wager anything that he will remember "Anthropophage" and hundreds of others just as difficult. Wonderful? No, not very. Like

Helen, he was able to communicate by feeling words spelt on his fingers, and there were very few who had the patience or inclination to talk with him. Therefore he could easily remember the little that was communicated to him. You who have all the five senses and are free to use them have such an infinite number of subjects to occupy your minds, and memory is strained to hold them all.

great →

My duties as companion were light and my leisure so ample that I could devote some of it to my favorite studies. One pleasant feature of my position was the opportunity granted me for calm, serene meditation. I was able to exercise my memory and pit experiences against facts and theories. As some of my conclusions bear upon this subject I shall take the liberty of presenting them.

There are a number of deaf-mutes whose sense of hearing is normal, but who cannot grasp the meaning of the articulated sounds and are incapable of imitating and speaking them. They are speechless in consequence. In tracing the cause of this strange defect, it has been ascertained that these deaf-mutes have not, during their childhood, come in contact and association with the hearing, hence their vocal cords, as well as their aural nerves, became atrophied. The best-equipped school for the deaf and the most skillful and conscientious teachers cannot help them any better than they can the true deaf-mutes. Many of the hard-of-hearing people carry small electric pocket devices and hear very well. They are constantly exercising their auditory nerves. The semi-mutes, with eardrums destroyed, and memories of what they have heard faded away, cannot be benefitted by instruments of any kind—not in the least.

To repeat, I lost my hearing when three years old, my eardrums, auditory nerves, put out of commission for all time. When thirty-five, I saw and tried a wonderful new apparatus which amplified and multiplied sound to any volume. It could make the pattering of a housefly resemble the trampling of a hundred mad elephants. The receiver was placed to my ears and the machine was adjusted to amplify the voice of a famous contralto. It sounded to me like the jangling, jarring, meaningless trampling of a hundred insane elephants pounding against my head. My ears could not catch a sound. The machine was next tuned to carry the fanfare of a brass band, and it sounded again like a series of giant blows against my head. The machine voiced the vowel "O," then "E," "I" and "U," but it was the same horde of crazy elephants all over again until my head ached. I could not tell one sound from another. After trying other machines, I refused absolutely to experiment further. It is as futile to try to describe sound to the stone-deaf as to explain colors and scenery to the born-blind.

In speaking of the blind, let me tell of a peculiarity that may be new to many of you. It is said that some people are born blind because of a film covering their eyes, called cataracts. Through skillful surgery some have been cured when fifteen, or even older; but, for a wonder, while they could see they could not understand what they saw. To them all objects looked alike in size, shape and color. Were a table, a clock, a book, or a pin put before them the "exblind" could not tell one from the other. But they could distinguish the objects by the sense of touch. They have learned to rely on this highly trained sense of touch. In the majority of totally blind, the optic nerve is dead, and in the deaf, it is the auditory nerves that are lifeless.

It may not be out of place here to mention one or two peculiarities: You may have contacted people with perfectly good eyes but who cannot distinguish colors; they are called "color blind." Or people who have good hearing, but who cannot differentiate tunes, and are called "tune-deaf."

❧14❧

THE SIGN LANGUAGE

To RETURN to Mr. Read, when I met him again he was business manager of the late Thomas H. Ince, director and producer. They had just arrived in New York to arrange for the Eastern premiere of "Civilization."

Mr. Ince took a lively interest in me, and he contemplated, for a moment, employing me as an actor in his company; but he changed his mind upon realizing that I could not hear the director's instructions. Thus, once more, the poor dummy missed another opportunity.

Of course, had the movie people troubled themselves to learn the sign language or, at least, the manual alphabet, this objection would have been removed. I shall leave it to you to conjecture why they didn't learn. Had they learned they would have realized its importance in picture making. A little serious thought on the subject might possibly have kept active the universal language that made motion pictures the entertainment of the world and have made unnecessary the sound devices that appear to have handicapped the screen.

Those who have witnessed the sign language as it is now used among most of the deaf say that it is too slovenly, even loathsome; an arraignment that is justified when referring to the uncultured, who, I regret to say, are too numerous among the deaf. Their abuse of the sign language is no different than the abuse of English that one finds among the hearing who use slang.

The prevalence of slang gives no valid reason for abolishing English as a language—nor should the crudities in the use of signs justify the banishment of the sign language.

Let me repeat once more that the **Sign Language cannot be, and never will be abolished.** Let me also repeat that the sign language is not responsible for any lack in the education of the deaf-mute—the pure oralists to the contrary not withstanding. Their efforts covering a century have been thoroughly tested and have been proved a failure. In fact they have helped to make me bitter, for I have been one of the victims.

To appraise the relative values of the sign language and the oral method, I undertook considerable research work. I will acquaint you with the results of my research and survey.

At public functions in different localities, I have asked some discerning person intimately acquainted with the deaf present to list those whom he believed capable of reading and writing as well as an average hearing person. On the average I found that out of every 100, about 20 were listed. In analyzing the 20, I found 15 semi-mutes and five deaf-mutes. The five were those who had left school about as early as I did, and who studied intensively afterwards. They were not graduates of schools using the pure-oral method. In my opinion, "there ain't no sich animal." Poor as this showing may be, I have been accused of having conferred too much credit on the schools.

The great majority, the 80 of the 100 could, communicate through the sign language. To them it was indeed a savior, for it leaped the barriers imposed by education and the many tongues of man. When conversing in the sign language the unlettered were on a level with the learned. The difference could be detected only when they took to **write or spell full phrases on their fingers.**

The experiences I have related should prove my contention that diseases, accidents, or congenitality do not impair the reasoning faculties of any deaf person. The inability to read and write proves nothing against his mentality. He stands on the same footing as any foreigner who can talk fluently in his own tongue, but cannot speak one word of English. It is, therefore, absurd to condemn as stupid a deaf-mute merely because he cannot talk in any tongue other than his own—the sign language. You would find many deaf-mutes mighty clever if you were to try to get the better of them in business. The chances are about even that you would get the worst of the bargain.

If you were to attend a gathering of the deaf and make a vocal address, to be translated into signs by a competent interpreter, you would remark how your deaf audience understood and enjoyed your lecture. They would be as generous in their response as they would had they heard your words. Furthermore, the interpreter would not interrupt you or lag behind.

I have known international Conventions of the Deaf where delegates from different countries were gathered. Their inability to "speak" their difficult tongues never interfered with smooth, complete, enjoyable communications. Neither did they need an interpreter; he would have been a hindrance, a nuisance, instead of help. They carried on their business with the same accuracy and dispatch as is done by any convention of the hearing talking in only **one** tongue. There are, sometimes, unusual, unfamiliar signs, different from ours; but the difference is slight and easily grasped, once it is explained.

❧15❧

THE SIGN LANGUAGE
BEAUTIFUL

FOR MANY years, more for amusement than for any serious purpose, I improvised some new features for the sign language. They
were along the lines of picture painting in the air. You may recall
what I said about the habit of deaf-mutes, from infancy, thinking
only in pictures. The transition from pictures to signs is, for me, so
smooth and natural that I always preferred signs to writing—a habit
from which I have never entirely broken away. In fact, I can always
express through signs in five minutes what would take me a whole
day of racking, mental wrestling to translate into words. In the end,
my words would not be one-tenth as graphic. To me self-expression
in words has been hopelessly difficult. I have found I am not the
only deaf-mute in this position.

When you learn the sign language, as I hope you will, you will
be astonished to find how much more readily you can express your
ideas. Words will seem slow and ponderous. When you become
an expert you will be able to spell the alphabet as fast manually
as orally.

The true sign language is nothing more or less than **drawing
pictures in the air.** A careless, slouchy sign maker will make poor
pictures with his hands, fingers, arms and facial expressions. A care-
fully trained "speaker" goes through his gestures deliberately and
artistically. His pictures then become plain and are pleasant to look

upon. The better he draws in the air, the more beautiful and more impressive become his pictures.

The pure sign language is as different from the slang as the awkward gambols of a waltzing elephant from the graceful, airy undulations of a Pavlowa.

In spite of the stifling atmosphere of institutional life, the deaf do not lose their instinct for rhythm. If you should attend a ball or social gathering of the deaf where dancing is indulged, you will be surprised to find a number of them going through a Fox Trot with grace and rhythm. Then you ask how they do it without hearing music. Someone may tell you that they feel vibrations through the floor. This in my opinion is sheer nonsense. They are guided solely by imagination and a latent sense of rhythm.

Many of the deaf are fond of rendering in signs, songs and hymns. They perform according to instinct, without training or coaching from artists. Lack of culture makes their "singing in signs" unsatisfactory. They believe they must "sign" the verses as they are printed—word for word. What they should do is to communicate ideas and not emasculate their expressions and emotions by an attempt to follow words.

Shortly before I married I became acquainted with a clever teacher of the Delsarte System of Expression and Pantomime. While there is no resemblance between it and the Sign Language of the Deaf, we both recognized good points in the two methods. We even undertook to blend the two. After some rehearsals we succeeded in a measure that won enthusiastic comment from hearing audiences.

I adopted this new combination as a child to raise and nurture. I improvised gestures that were a combination of the language of the deaf and the "signs" of the Indians, Italians, French, etc. I tried to make them take the form of well-defined pictures, without sacrificing expression or emotion. My aim was to make them intelligible to everyone, even to those who never had seen stories rendered in signs.

64

By the time my oldest child reached her eighth year, I had taught her to sing in signs the hymn "Nearer, My God to Thee," using the sign method that I had worked out. I made her blend one gesture into another until every verse resembled what we might call "visible music." It was not dissimilar to the rhythm of Greek dancing.

Confident that she could render the hymn in public, I had her "speak" at a few Church gatherings of the hearing. As to the results, I will quote from articles that appeared in newspapers:

> The most impressive rendering of "Nearer, My God, to Thee" that the writer has ever witnessed was by little Marion Ballin. I have seen it rendered by past masters of Delsartan gestures, and of our own beautiful language of signs, but none has approached the reverential beauty and grace given by little Miss Ballin.
> —*Deaf-Mutes Journal*, May, 1905.

> I have heard from a dozen different sources how a little, eight-year old girl, the hearing daughter of a deaf-mute father, an unusually gifted sign maker and brilliant thinker, and the mother, also a gifted woman and a highly rated musician, made an audience gasp in astonishment when she recited in signs, the hymn, "Nearer, My God, to Thee," accompanied on the piano by her mother. Those who saw the really wonderful exhibition say that they never saw anything like it before, and that no deaf-mute, to whom the language of signs comes most natural, ever approached her in grace, ease or clearness.

> But it is not to be wondered at, for the child inherits from her parents all the characteristics of both. She makes signs as graphically as her father does, from the music her mother furnished, she infused melody into her expression. Fragment of an article by Alexander L. Pach, in the *Silent Worker*, June, 1905.

On other occasions I recited songs, such as "Lochinvar," "Star-Spangled Banner," etc. In paraphrasing "The Marseillaise" I chose the original French version by Captain Rouget de l'Isle. I believe I succeeded in my attempt to make of it a real motion picture. You

Albert Ballin and Laura La Plante "talk" with one another
on the set of *La Marseillaise*.

know that a painting on canvass, if skillfully executed, needs no translation into any other language. It is a poor artist who has to put on a label.

The following quotations speak for themselves:

Mr. Ballin's hands flashed with a dramatic gesture as he opened the meeting with "The Marseillaise" in the sign language. He rocked the babe in his arms and rolled up the tyrant in a ball and cast him out from the stage with such violence that a little man chewing a cigar in the front row nearly swallowed the butt in his terror.

Mr. Ballin called the citizens together with a magnificent sweep of his hand that thrilled the audience and ended with a vivid piece of acting which brought a burst of applause from his listeners.—*New York Call*, October, 1921.

And after the banquet, Mrs. Terry introduced a visitor from New York, Albert Ballin, a brilliantly dramatic deaf-mute, who kept them in ecstasies of delight with his busy fingers, and "sang" them "The Marseillaise" with such dramatic gestures that I vow I could hear the marching feet, the beating of the drums, the war cries of the French, and see the flag in the breeze.

The "speaker" also had considerable to say about the numerous signs and gestures of the directors, actors and their hearing audiences, which often mean something different to the deaf. He considered it the duty of the industry to study the language of the deaf—many of which are infinitely more interpretive of the real emotions than the forms now in use to portray the silent drama. Alma Whitaker, in the *Los Angeles Times*, May 11, 1924.

❧§16§❧

THE GREAT UNSCHOOLED

You are probably aware that the inability to read and write is not confined to the deaf. It is in certain sections of this country all too common among the hearing. But I found that those hearing people who could neither read nor write were not always lacking intelligence. It did, however, seem strange to me that such a condition could exist in a country which is supposed to have one of the best school systems in the world.

My curiosity was aroused by a statement believed to be made by General Pershing while he was abroad during the Great War. I came across it somewhere, I cannot recall exactly when or where; but I saw it, and it ate deeply into my memory. In the statement he is supposed to have said that out of all the drafted men sent to him, only forty percent of them could read and write. It is not easy to understand how this could have happened when the draft was selective. But regardless of whether or not this statement was made, it did lead to my undertaking an investigation of my own.

It was a long, dreary trail for me to follow; so obscure, so elusive, so baffling. I had to dig into Census Reports, School Reports, Statistics of Attendance to Libraries, Circulations of Newspapers, "best-sellers" among books, and similar sources of information, until I became dizzy. Such research is as dry as dust, and as uninteresting as a Patent Office Report—and a darned sight more troublesome. Assuming that your tastes are similar to mine, I shall not pester you with details of my investigations. You will have to accept my word that what I found convinced me that the statement attributed to General Pershing was probably true. If you want details you will have to search them out for yourself. I am getting on in years, and I wish to devote the few years still left to me to pursuits more pleasant than being choked and finally buried by statistics.

I am embarrassed in choosing an appropriate name for that class who cannot read or write. I mean those who are intelligent and capable of understanding and expressing themselves orally— the same as intelligent deaf-mutes who use signs. I cannot, in fairness, call them illiterate as defined by the dictionary: unlettered, ignorant of books or letters, untaught, unlettered, uninstructed in science. Unschooled is no more just. Though, **faut de mieux,** I put this title to this chapter—with apologies. Perhaps I can make my meaning plainer in the following paragraphs.

There are an enormous number of people who understand what is said to them and who are able to make themselves understood orally. Sometimes they mix their vernacular with foreign tongues or dialects. But in spite of this condition they get along famously in life and business, and are very worthy citizens. I know personally wealthy contractors, builders, and bankers who can scribble only their names on the dotted line on their checks and contracts. I daresay that you, too, have met with these rare specimens of humanity. It is really impossible to number these people, for they are most successful in hiding their weakness as writers and readers behind shrewd eloquence. Whenever I meet them, and try to talk with them in writing, they point to their eyes to signify that their sight is defective. They beckon someone else to come and help carry on conversation with me—and then cross over to the other side of the street when they see me a second time. They are too proud to confess their so-called illiteracy, even to the census taker. Command of English is, in my opinion, an unreliable yardstick with which to measure a person's mental caliber.

Another fact we have to take into consideration is the presence in our midst of a great number of foreigners who can't or won't learn English. In an early part of this book I told of the difficulties faced by one undertaking to master a foreign language. I except, of course, the gifted highbrows. But they are a small proportion of the populace.

There have been times when I had qualms of doubt about the necessity of a command of written language, when we have within reach the simplest, most natural, easiest understood, least ambiguous language in the world.

Benjamin Disraeli said: "Man uses language to conceal his real thoughts." Mark Twain declaimed more bluntly that, "the first use man made of language was to tell lies."

These men, I believe, had in mind when they penned the lines just quoted diplomats, statesmen and some lawyers.

Their idea may explain the adage, "Children and fools tell the truth."

ꞏ17ꞏ

COMING TO CALIFORNIA

WITH HIGH hopes and ambition, I packed what little I possessed in worldly goods into my grip and boarded the good ship *Finland* to sail for California, the home of our beloved Cinema Child.

Some deaf friends came to wave me God-speed on my hazardous venture. Here I must mention a feature that is often seen, but whose significance is seldom considered. As the ship was unmoored and started on her long voyage, her passengers and their friends on the dock were yelling their parting farewells, using their hands as megaphones; but all their vocal exchanges were drowned by the steam sirens, clanging bells, stentorian orders of the ship officers, shouts of the seamen and the general bedlam. My deaf friends and I were never harassed by this ear-splitting clamor. For us it did not exist. We went on conversing, using our fingers and arms, missing not one word. I believe the last message I flashed off on my fingers was: "You can see that our deafness is a blessing in disguise. Now we have the laugh on the hearing and can pity their helplessness? What?"

Came the answer: "Right you are, old man! Bon voyage and good luck to you!"

Our conversation was soon cut short by the warping of the ship around to the other side. We could have gone on talking at a distance far beyond ear-shot. Our system was far better than that of the signal wig-wagging of sailors on a warship.

I now propose to plunge into an account of my adventures in the motion picture world.

I received a splendid welcome at the Ince Studio (now Pathe). Mr. Ince knew and appreciated my purpose in coming and gave me complete freedom of the studio and facilities to study all details at close range. I visited other studios where I was welcomed and assisted in my work. From that time dates my affiliation with the industry. I served as a writer for periodicals and magazines, teacher of signs to the acting fraternity, and as a painter of portraits. At various times I was used as an actor in minor bits. In fact, were I to permit myself to digress, I could fill several volumes with accounts of my interesting experiences.

One of the most striking curiosities, a downright anomaly in this industry, is the utter lack of directors who can talk fluently on their fingers. I searched diligently and found only one. He spells slowly and rheumatically on his fingers, and no more. All the directors I have met are friendly, very fine gentlemen, supremely clever in their work. Nevertheless, it does look odd from my point of view that they should not know this sign language—**the language so necessary to picture-making.**

With the exception of two or three actors, like the late Lon Chaney, who are children of deaf-mute parents, practically everyone connected with the industry, from the highest producer down to the lowly sweeper, is blissfully (?) ignorant of the sign language. Lon Chaney declared in published articles that he was thankful for his knowledge of signs and believed that much of his success was due to that knowledge.

In watching the production of pictures, I noticed a great deal of waste in time and money because of this lack of knowledge of signs. The following is an illustration:

I witnessed a scene where the heroine was fleeing in an automobile. She was crouching at the wheel, turning her head every minute or two to watch her pursuers. The car was actually at a standstill. In the background was a canvas with pictures of fields, trees, shrubbery, telegraph poles, turning swiftly on revolving cylinders, to give the illusion that the car was moving. To intensify the illusion, four men, two at either end, jumped up and down on planks attached to the car, making it appear as if the car were driving along a rough road. In front of the car out of camera range, a motor-driven propeller blew wind at the car, fluttering the heroine's hair and ribbons in the breeze. The illusion of the car rushing at full speed turned out perfectly on the screen. By an oversight, the girl's hair and ribbons were stuck fast inside her coat. The director bellowed directions through his megaphone, ordering her to loosen her ribbons; but the din created by the aeroplane machine was too deafening for her to hear him. He had to stop the camera, walk up to her, and explain what he wanted and then make a retake.

At the conclusion, I wrote on my pad. You are a h— of a director. If you knew how, you could have made signs to the girl to loosen her hair and be spared the retake.

The director, a good-natured friend, glared at me; then his scowling features melted into a broad grin. He nodded that I was just in my criticism.

I also saw mob scenes, cowboys and soldiers shooting guns, houses on fire, battle scenes and other scenes that produced terrific din, drowning all vocal orders. In the handling of such scenes, signs would have been invaluable.

The time may come when we shall have no more use for directors or players who are ignorant of the sign language than we would for carpenters who don't know the use of a hammer or saw.

At a certain studio, during a dissertation on my favorite topic, I made some remarks characterizing the bulk of motion pictures as rank bunk, insulting to the intelligence of the American people. One actor laughingly declared that "stories are written by, of, and for dumb-bells." The director retorted, "about eighty percent of the American people are morons, the class that pays and supports the movies; we have put across some high-brow stuff (naming several truly great stories), and they were financial failures." Another actor nodded gravely and added, "We have to cater to the tastes of the morons or go out of business altogether."

Albert Ballin in the silent movie, *His Busy Hour*.

There is a good deal of sense in these remarks, when viewed from the old, unsound theory that most people are low in mentality and tastes. But the accusation is erroneous. I must repeat my conclusions that the great majority of the people are really intelligent, but too many, about sixty percent, are "unschooled" in the sense I have already defined.

Those who cannot read the words thrown on the screen lose the story—they become disgusted and bored, and, thereafter refuse to see such shows. This has been plainly proved by the crowds that flock to see Charlie Chaplin's pictures. Those he made fifteen years ago are popular today. They are pictures—not words. The bunk offered by some producers will always keep away self-respecting spectators who can read. Ignoring the fundamental causes of diminishing box-office receipts, many producers have the idea that they can repair the damage by offering pictures that are sillier and more salacious. They act like the man who fell into quicksand—the harder he struggled the faster he would sink. Hence the poor Cinema is becoming anaemic and sickly.

There has boomed suddenly into our midst an innovation called the Talkie, which reproduces the human voice, music and all sounds. The producers and exhibitors have scrambled after it headlong, spending hundreds of millions with a lavish hand. Though far from perfected, the device, like a mother-in-law, is likely to remain with us. Now that oral speech has reached the screen, it is expected to help the box office. It may for a time—but will it last? Will the success be permanent? I doubt it. We are still in a hysterical mood, a natural sequence after the Great War. The instant success of the "Talkie" does, however, show the need of a substitute for the endless words that formerly were written on the screen. Speech does help a goodly number of the so-called "unschooled." It also succeeds in driving away all the deaf and hard-of-hearing. And how these bemoan the passing of the silent movie. It was counted among their few blessings. It entertained and helped to keep them cheerful. "But it brings in the blind," remarked a publicity man to me. Smart of him, perhaps, but he forgets that the deaf pay admission fees; the blind don't.

The "Talkie" restricts theater attendance to those understanding the one language. It turns away those to whom the tongue is foreign. It may be all right, even commendable, to utilize music and all other appropriate sounds to enhance illusions of reality, but we can very well eliminate monologues, dialogues and all orally spoken words that have to be translated into many tongues to reach the world. At best, dialogue retards and slows down action, one of the greatest charms of motion pictures. The Cinema will fall short of its idea if it does not make itself universal; and it can never be universal unless it is understood everywhere on the globe.

We have been living in the jazz age too long; we are exhausted, sick of the incessant clamor worthy only of savages. Does the Talkie threaten us with more just when we are beginning to yearn after repose?

When we sit down to read and enjoy a story, the book in our hands does not shriek from every page with all varieties of type-screaming capitals, italics, copious foot-notes. It would irritate and disgust us and we would throw it into the fireplace. A good story is best when couched in plain, clean type, clearly and simply phrased, leaving plenty of room for imagination. Many of the old silent pictures have been eminently successful; they linger in our memories like good books. It is the kind of work that we ought to preserve and improve.

Charlie Chaplin, the famous comedian, knows a good deal about the signs and makes excellent use of them without making of them a distinct language. You never see him open his mouth to utter one syllable; his sub-titles are few and short. We know he regrets having to use any at all. His pictures are, in consequence, never in need of translation. From them he has made a fortune that he well deserves.

As I was penning the above lines, I came across an article

Stills of Albert Ballin from the silent movie, *His Busy Hour.*

entitled, "Charlie Chaplin Attacks the Talkies." It appears in the magazine, *Motion Pictures,* for May, 1929. I am quoting from it:

> You can tell 'em I loathe them [he said]. They are spoiling the oldest art in the world—the art of pantomime. They are ruining the great beauty of silence. They are defeating the meaning of the screen, the appeal that has created the star system, the fan system, the vast popularity of the whole—the appeal of beauty. . . . It is beauty that matters in pictures—nothing else. The screen is pictorial. Pictures . . . I am not using the talkies in my new picture. I am never going to use them. For me, it would be fatal. I can't understand why anyone who can possibly avoid it, does use it; Harold Lloyd, for instance.

Mr. Chaplin knows his subject thoroughly and can speak about it with authority. Frankly, I count him one of the staunchest supporters of the movement this book proposes to launch. We need the influence of a few more men like him to help overcome the ignorance and baseless prejudices that handicap progress.

In speaking of the ignorance on this subject, let me separate it from the indifference that is responsible for what the deaf-mute is and for woes that pursue him throughout his whole life. To make clear the presence of this ignorance among those supposed to possess intelligence, I will relate an experience in one of the studios where I met many who were most learned, and generous.

When I first met the very charming Miss Betty Compson, she asked me, during an interview, "Can you read the lips?"

I answered, "No, I can't."

"Why not?" she demanded.

My reply was, "Can you spell on your fingers?"

"No," came the quick response.

I smiled, as I repeated her own words, "Why not?"

"Why should I?" she asked. "I never meet any deaf people."

When I did not answer she continued, "Let me tell you that I have a very dear friend who is a great actress on both the stage and screen. She was so sensitive when her hearing became affected that she learned to read lips so well that nobody knows about her trouble. Her name is Louise D—."

I felt like saying, "Oh, Louise, how can you read the lips when your back is turned, or when the kleig lights are in your eyes? How can you read the lips of your director when his mouth is hidden behind a megaphone? It is difficult enough for anyone to pretend to be a deaf-mute; but for a deaf person to conduct herself as one who hears—well, it has me stumped." But I could not embarrass sweet Betty with inquiries along such lines.

"That is very fine," I replied, "How old was she when her hearing began to fail?"

"I am not sure. Perhaps thirty."

"You see," I explained, "she could hear and talk like you until she was thirty, and then lipreading was all she had to learn. You don't seem to realize that it takes a deaf child fifteen, twenty, sometimes twenty-five years of hardest labor, and the sacrifice of all other branches of learning, to even attempt to talk orally and to read the lips. Even after years of study and work he is likely to fail in the end. All these years are given to save **you and those like you** some thirty minutes of your whole life. Is it fair to ask this of the deaf when a few minutes would enable you to spell on your fingers and communicate with him?"

Betty looked surprised and pained. She turned to speak with her friends. Then she wrote on my pad with tears trickling down the pencil point: "We never looked at the thing in that light before. I am so ashamed of myself and beg your pardon."

Like most others, she was merely ignorant of this much-slighted subject. I meet others like her every day, innocent and perfectly sincere in asking me the same questions—never suspecting that they are asking a question no less absurd than, "Can you dance blindfolded on a swinging rope on a stormy night?"

It has taken me a year to compile this book after almost a lifetime of careful thinking. During the years I have repeatedly been asked the question that was put to me by Miss Compson. It is rather discouraging.

When I first met Mary Pickford, she also asked me this heart-breaking question, "Can you read the lips?" I hope to be forgiven for replying, "No, I only kiss them when they are sweet like yours." Of course, she excused me by laughing merrily.

❧18❧

BENEFITS TO THE DEAF

I TRUST I convinced you, by presenting facts and proofs, that the Universal Sign Language would be a help to mankind. Further discussion seems needless, so I will offer a few prognostications as to probable results were it in effect.

First, let us calculate its value to the deaf-mutes, out of whose sufferings was borne the **Idea.** (Also the telephone.)

When **everybody** can talk in the sign language it will be unnecessary to send any deaf child to the established schools and institutes for the deaf and doom him to all their inherent miseries. Instead, he will be sent to the school for the hearing children that is nearest to his home. **With the teachers and hearing scholars already familiar with the sign language, he will be well taken care of.**

At first he may be a little backward. This is to be expected. But by constant association with hearing children, and incessant spelling on his fingers, he will acquire the habit of **thinking** in words, and mastery of good English will follow naturally. He will catch up with his schoolmates, and if bright, he may outdo them in his studies. This would be quite possible because of the ease of concentration due to his affliction.

There is the possibility that you, who read this book, may have reason to contact a deaf child. Your knowledge of the sign language would then be of inestimable value, for you could help him with his studies. Were the child yours you could teach him until he reached school age. Such early instruction would develop his mind.

Furthermore, by keeping him from other deaf-mutes, he would not acquire their peculiarities. His mind would not be a blank insofar as words are concerned. Later, he would not care to limit his acquaintances to his fellow unfortunates. He would be an equal with the hearing and feel at home everywhere; just as I did while in Italy among sign-making people.

In short, he would be like his hearing brethren in all particulars except his inability to hear and speak orally. He would merge into the population, and his impediment would seldom be noticed.

With the exception of those few who lose their hearing late in life, the deaf do not bemoan their loss. Edison is deaf, but he wastes no time or thought in maudlin moaning over his deafness. On the contrary, he considers it a blessing for he hears no evil noises, and it keeps his mind directed upon the things that really count. **We never miss what we never had.**

Before closing this chapter, I wish to refresh your memory concerning my agreement with Dr. Bell on his brilliant idea of razing the existing schools for the deaf—the idea he never carried out. I would suggest a method of carrying it out that would not need the passing of a single law to carry on the pleasant work of destruction, nor would it cost anyone one cent. It would be to have the world of the hearing learn the Universal Language of Signs. That alone will attain the long-sought-after goal. The attendance of the deaf children at schools for the hearing would automatically close the schools built for the deaf, and they could then be put to some use that would, I hope, prove more constructive.

❧§19❧

BENEFITS TO OTHERS

EARLIER IN this little volume I mentioned how the deaf hold International Conventions where the delegates "speak" with ease and without the aid of interpreters. Let us compare these conventions with the frequent meetings of ambassadors, ministers, or delegates of foreign nations. For a concrete example, let us select the Disarmament Conference, held, not long ago, at Washington, D.C. There, a brilliant French diplomat delivered a stirring address in his native tongue, but he had to stop every few minutes for his interpreter to translate it into English. French is rich in idioms and capable of delicate differences of meaning that would tax the ability of the cleverest translators to do it justice in another tongue. When the address was translated into English, the delegates from the other nations had to sit with frozen faces and stare blankly ahead like a deaf-mute at a musicale—and be just as unhappy. Many days lapsed before the addresses could be translated into the many languages represented by the delegates. Delays of this sort can be very dangerous, especially in matters of diplomacy. Such conferences must appear cumbersome—even silly, in comparison with those of the deaf. Were the speeches at the conferences of the hearing interpreted by one who could speak through signs, much time would be saved. This is done at the pow-wow among different Indian tribes.

The sign language would be a convenience in bringing about silence among the chattering at the opera, theater and concert. If they insisted upon being noisy, you would then feel justified in throwing them out bodily.

In restaurants, the waiters could give and receive orders in silence, and leave you to concentrate on the gentle cadences of hot
soup gurgling down the capacious throat of a big Mack Swain.

How I love to watch the work on a new steel structure soaring
to the sky. The great cranes pick up heavy steel girders, hoist them
up and up, swing them around, and fit them into place, without
loss of time, and without confusion. I can feel the vibrations thundering at my feet and imagine that a terrific clamor is going on with
sledgehammers rising and falling, pneumatic riveters throbbing—a
din deafening enough to make the deaf hear. This bedlam of noise
does not confuse the workers or stop their communicating with
one another. Why? Because the workers make signs to each other.
The engineer at his winch watches intently a worker who whirls
his forefinger for "up, up." When the worker stretches his arms hor-
izontally it means "stop." The next moment his right thumb jerks
to the right to indicate the direction the crane must turn. A gentle
rising of the right thumb under the left palm for the slow raising of
the girder, inch by inch, and so on until the job of placing the girder
is completed. To the uninitiated the crane seems to be endowed
with life and human intelligence.

Suddenly the workers stop and stretch their necks to see what's
going on in the street below. Crowds of people are being pushed
back by policemen to leave a wide path for the dashing red streaks
that are fire engines. The excitement of a fire has never left me, so
I run after the engines, my blood tingling. The fire is five blocks
east. I climb a lamppost and roost on its sharp point to obtain an
unobstructed view of the exciting scene ahead.

The hose is attached in a matter of seconds; the ladders are
swung aloft, and firemen climb rapidly toward a group of fright-
ened, yelling women and children at a window. Some are bereft of
reason and jump to the ground but are saved by the nets stretched,
ready to catch them. Children cry, dogs bark, and the motley
crowd shrieks.

The battalion chief, a cool-headed veteran, calmly surveys the whole situation. He has discarded his speaking trumpet as a useless relic of antiquity. He uses clear, unmistakable gestures in giving orders to the firemen posted on the top of the blazing tenement. He tells them to go into the back room on the third floor to carry out a blind old granny and her crippled little granddaughter. He warns others to jump to the other side, for the partition wall is going to crumple in a second. The firemen understand and obey him perfectly. Shortly the fire is under control, the people saved, and the hubbub subsides.

This fire is only a pipe dream of mine. It did not happen in this way. But it can, and may, some day. Quién sabe?

I stood on a street corner near Pershing Square watching Sergeant Cleaves waving directions to hurrying cars and foot-passengers.

All at once he frowned ominously. He had seen a persistent flouter of the regulations attempting to sneak around the corner at the forbidden moment. He made signs to the effect, "If yer won't stop right where yer be, I'll cut out yer appendix! Move back pronto, will yer?" To another culprit, he signed, "If yer ain't keerful, yer'll get ninety-nine years in the hoosegow. See?"

Soon, along comes a former school teacher of the oral method for the deaf. He could not endure the signs made by the officer. He strode up and began his pompous harangue. Being deaf and a dud at lipreading, I could not catch on to the exact words he delivered, but at the subsequent inquest they were recorded somewhat like this:

It is my bounden duty, my dear Sir, at this grievous juxtaposition, to assume my prerogative as a propounder of the transcendent palladium of the American Intellectuality, and the sublime attitudes of our time-honored and cherished pedagogy to protest this unwarranted, obtrusive presumption to introduce those inconvertible, brain-corroding gesticulations of our pre-historical anthropophagic antecedents from whom we are supposed to have descended. Although this misapprehended theory has not been academically adjudicated as a substitute or rather a super-supposition in contradistinctability of—

Here the long-winded harangue was abruptly, pitilessly cut short. The officer, for the first (and last) time lost his balance. His ruddy color vanished, and he went ghastly white. His Irish ire was aroused. All he knew was that he was up against something beyond his understanding, or, as he picturesquely expressed himself at the inquest, "That crazy guy was off his nut. He blocked traffic. I could-nt edge in one wurrud. I'd to stop him one way or other accordin' to me lights of me dooty!"

Hence, the explanation of the crashing blow of the officer's billy—the kind that might have caved in the skull of an ox. But the ex-teacher was not badly hurt. He was saved by the wondrous thickness and hardness of his head. With but a lump on his poll, he came out sound physically, and unchanged—mentally speaking—as is to be expected of him and his tribe.

⁊❧20❧⁊

HOW TO LEARN IT

UPON THE assumption that you are, by this time, in accord with my ideas, you may ask what you can do to learn the **Universal Language** and use it to remedy the ills I have mentioned.

The first and most important step is to learn the single-hand manual alphabet, plainly illustrated here. Imitate the way the letters are formed from A to Z, also the &. Spell each letter clearly. Do not move your hand around or crook your fingers clumsily as if they were stiff. Do not lift or lower your hand jerkily while spelling each letter or word. When you do, you make your "listener" move his head rapidly to follow you. Watch out—he may dislocate his neck. If you spell awkwardly or carelessly, it will be as difficult to read your words as deciphering the hieroglyphics on the obelisk. Do not make any gesture between the words, just pause an instant or two in passing from one word to another, the same as you space them in talking orally. Always keep your hand immovable, and let only your fingers do the work.

You have only twenty-six letters to learn, not thousands of new words of a foreign language and its grammar, a task that requires years of toil. After you have mastered your manual alphabet, repeat it many times; you will be surprised with your own ease and fluency.

When you have the manual alphabet on your fingertips, so to speak, you will have accomplished more than half—fully seventy-five percent. The next step is to make your friends learn it in exactly the same way; then talk with them only on the fingers. It is more difficult to read others' fingers than to use your own. It is a matter of a few days practice to do it well. When alone, it is excellent practice to watch your fingers in a mirror; almost as good as studying your friends'.

The sign language is altogether different from the manual alphabet, for it uses gestures or pictures in the air. It can be learned from those who make simple, clear signs. Be careful in selecting your teacher, because if you begin making wrong or poor signs it will be difficult to change them afterwards. Begin right. There are among the deaf, especially the ladies, many who can teach conversational signs. The best teachers are children of deaf parents. Their ability to talk orally helps them in explaining the reason and meaning of every gesture. There are many who will gladly teach you for the love of it.

It is my hope that the Cinema Industry will start a school where a standardized Code will be taught, and accepted the world over.

The children at public schools learn easily. It would be effective for them to use the sign language as a part of their daily exercise, the same as gymnastics. A page of the manual alphabet should be put in the school textbooks. A law to this effect is all that would be required to bring into existence the Universal Language.

The sign language can be developed to a degree of artistry considerably above the conversational style. In such form it may be used for silent singing, dramatic expression and similar purposes. To attain perfection in the Art one must be willing to study and practice. Like dancing, everyone who walks can learn it; but it is not everyone who can dance like Pavlowa.

It is the duty of the motion picture actor to strive for perfection in this Art. Such effort is necessary, not only for clear understanding, but also to help elevate the tone of sign-making among the masses. In the wake will follow better, finer pictures, and greater attendance at the theaters.

It takes but a slight effort to visualize the ultimate results of the usage of the Universal Language, the new understanding among all

Harry Burns (right), editor of *Hollywood Filmographer,* making the sign for "wild bull with crooked horns" after learning the sign for "cow."

races and nations. The better we know our neighbors, the more we shall love them. It will help to bring peace on the earth, and good will to man.

The only ones who will protest against this "innovation" are the pure oralists, the beneficiaries of the institutions for the deaf, and other parasites who prey on the misfortunes of the deaf. They comprise but a small portion of the human race. In one respect, they resemble the celebrated cow of Robert Stephenson. Do you know the story?

When Stephenson's proposition to introduce his steam locomotive into traffic in England was before Parliament, a member asked him, "Would it not be bad if a cow should stand on the track?"

"Ya-as," drawled Stephenson. "Vera bad for the coo."

APPENDIX

IT WAS several years after I completed and laid aside the manuscript of this book that I heard of the existence of other treatises on the sign language by eminent authorities. I read a most admirable one, *The Sign Talk,* with 700 illustrations, by the renowned hunter, artist, and author Ernest Thompson Seton. It treats of the North American Indian's Sign Language, and makes many references to the language of the deaf. What surprised and delighted me was the fact that the views advanced by Mr. Seton were in harmony with my own. How I did envy his magnificent command of English—so limpid and convincing. I cannot recommend too emphatically a study of his book to all who contemplate learning the Indian Sign Language. (Publishers are Doubleday, Page & Co., 1917.)

I feel sure that a reproduction of at least a few pages from Mr. Seton's work will add strength to the claims I have made. Having had the pleasure of meeting Mr. Seton and actually chatting with him by means of signs, I found him agreeable to my quoting from his book.

Following are the paragraphs I selected. The paragraphs quoted are Mr. Seton's own:

Many thoughtful men have been trying for a century, at least, to give mankind a world speech which would overstep all linguistic barriers, and one cannot help wondering why they have overlooked the Sign Language, the one made common to mankind, already established and as old as Babel. Yes, more ancient than the hills.

APPENDIX

A true Sign Language is an established code of logical gestures to convey ideas; and is designed as an appeal to the eye, without the assistance of sounds, grimaces, apparatus, personal contact, written or spoken languages, or reference to words or letters; preferably made by using only the hands and adjoining parts of the body.

1st.   **It develops observation and accurate thinking.** All races that excel in sign-talking are noted for their keenness of observation. Which is cause and which is effect one cannot determine, but it is certain that the method of communication is excellent practice to develop observation, and it makes for wonderfully graphic descriptive power.

Herein, perhaps, is its most enduring, and least obvious claim to a high place. There is a sweet reasonableness, a mathematical accuracy, in the fabric of the Sign Language that has an insistent and reactionary effect on the mental processes and pictures of those who use it. Therefore, it is valuable for the kind of mind it makes.

2nd.   **It is easily learned.** Unlike most languages it very easily acquired, for most of the signs are natural in concept, and so logical that they explain themselves where their history is known. Six hundred signs (that is ideas) make a fairly good sign talker.

3rd.   **It is Indian Talk.** By means of this you can talk to any Plains Indian no matter what his speech; and there are many tribes each with its own tongue or dialect. In some measure it is understood and used by savages and keen observers all over the globe.

4th.   **A cognate code is the talk of the deaf; and is used the world round by them** in preference to the manual alphabet when possible, so that a wide use of the much better Indian Sign Language will certainly result in their accepting it and thus lessen the barrier between the deaf and their more fortunate brethren.

5th.   **It is silent talk.** It can be used on occasion when it is necessary to give information, but improper or impossible to speak aloud. Thus, lecturers use it in directing their lanternist; friends use it for necessary information during musical performances; it is used at the bedside of the sick, the actors in a moving picture can utilize it, and so be comprehended the world round; the pantomime stage, forbidden to use speech, can easily clear the plot by sign-talk.

In a recent letter, Prof. J. S. Long has furnished me with a touching instance (one that has since recurred) that indicates another and final service that the silent method can render.[1] An eminent divine was on his deathbed. His life had been devoted to ministering to the deaf, he knew the Sign Language perfectly; for several hours before the end his power of ordinary speech had deserted him, but his mind was clear, and to the last he conversed freely with those about him, in this, the universal language, the one which for its exercise depended on muscular powers that in his case were the last of all to fail.

6th. **It allows talk in an uproar.** It can be used when great noise makes it impossible to use the voice; therefore it can be of daily service in modern life, city or country, and each year it discovers new uses. Friends talk across a rackety thoroughfare or from a moving train; sailors in a storm find it serves them. The baseball umpire uses it when the roar of the multitude makes him voiceless; the catcher talks to the pitcher; the aeroplanist talks to his friends on earth; the stockbroker on the curb buys and sells in it; the football captain, or the army officer, issues clear sign orders when the uproar of the fight would drown even the trumpet call. The politician facing a shrieking mob finds it useful.

7th. **It is practical far-talk.** It is a valuable method of talking at a distance, far beyond earshot. Compared with the other modes of far-signaling it has the great advantage of speed, for it gives a sentence, while semaphore, Morse or Myer Code, give a letter; and of inconspicuousness at short range, or in a crowd. Also, it is independent of apparatus.

8th. **It is a true universal language.** It is already established. Instinctively the whole world has adopted it in a measure; and daily proof of this is seen. Rasmussen tells us he would have been helpless among the Eskimo, were it not that they were expert sign-makers,

---

1. Joseph Schuyler Long was a graduate of Gallaudet College, principal of the Iowa School for the Deaf in the early twentieth century, and author of *The Sign Language: A Manual of Signs* (Washington, D.C.: Press of Gibson Brothers, 1910). *Ed.*

and the linguistic barrier was swept away. The same is true of Henry among the Mandans, and Butler among the Basutos.

The language is so complete that Dr. W. C. Roe and many others regularly **preach** and **lecture** in the language of Signs. Their congregations are made up of people who speak several tongues and an interpreter would be necessary were the preacher limited to sounds.

The language is so fundamental that it is the easiest means of communicating with animals; the best trainers of dogs and horses use Sign Language as the principal medium of command.

But, for lack of standards and codification, its use is less than what it might be; yet larger than commonly supposed. After the extension of study, which will surely follow the adopting of a standard code, one will be able to travel all over Europe and use Sign Language alone. No matter what the other man's language may be, French, German, Russian, Greek, all are one in the Sign Language because it expresses ideas, not words. This, then, is its special strength.

"IT IS A UNIVERSAL LANGUAGE."